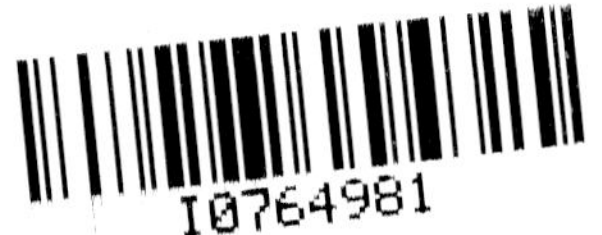

Coloring book for adults and kids amazing giant image for design

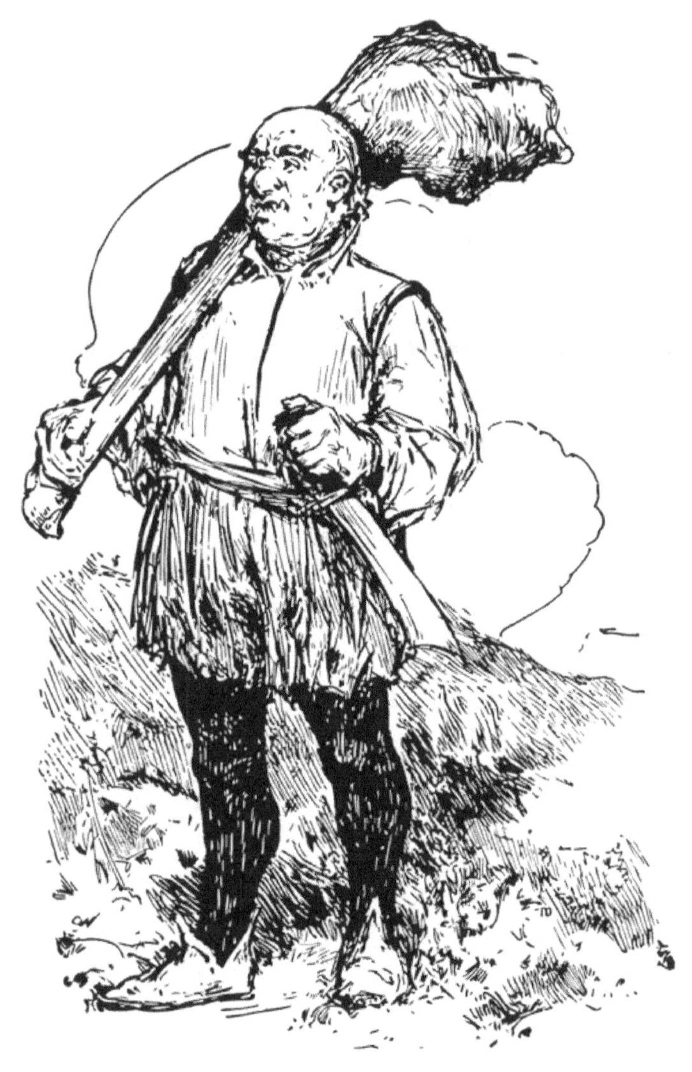

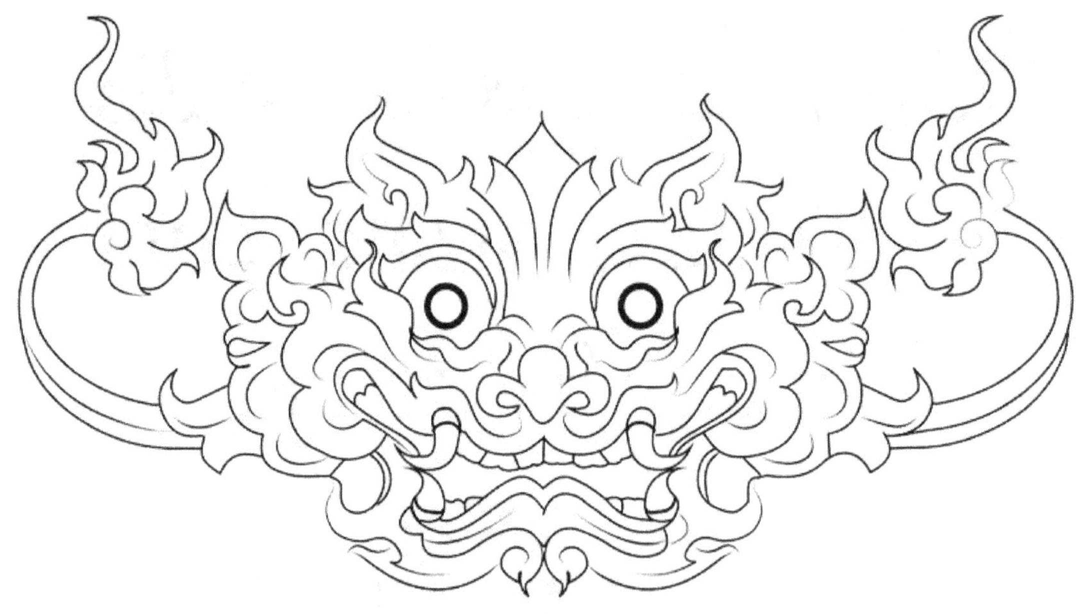

This coloring book is

belongs to

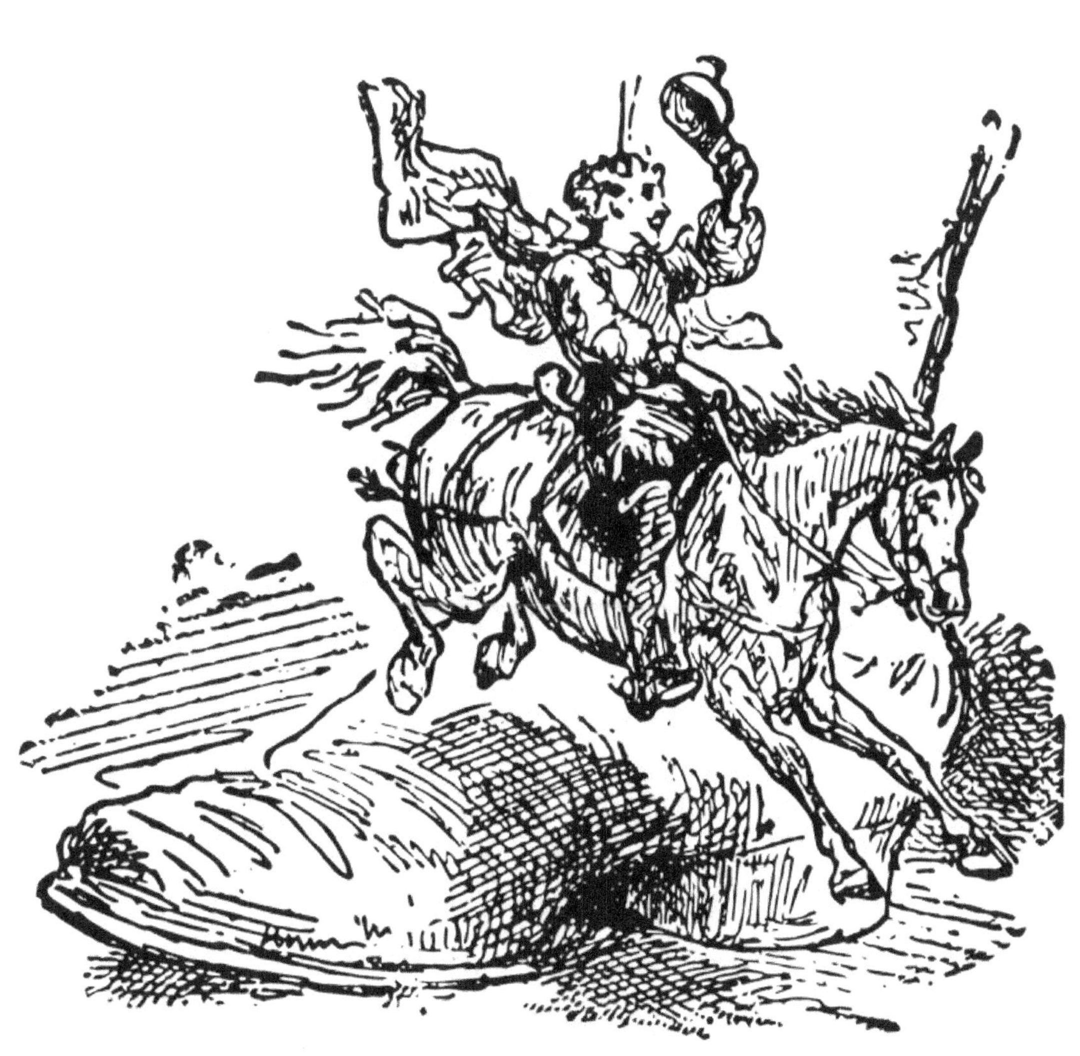

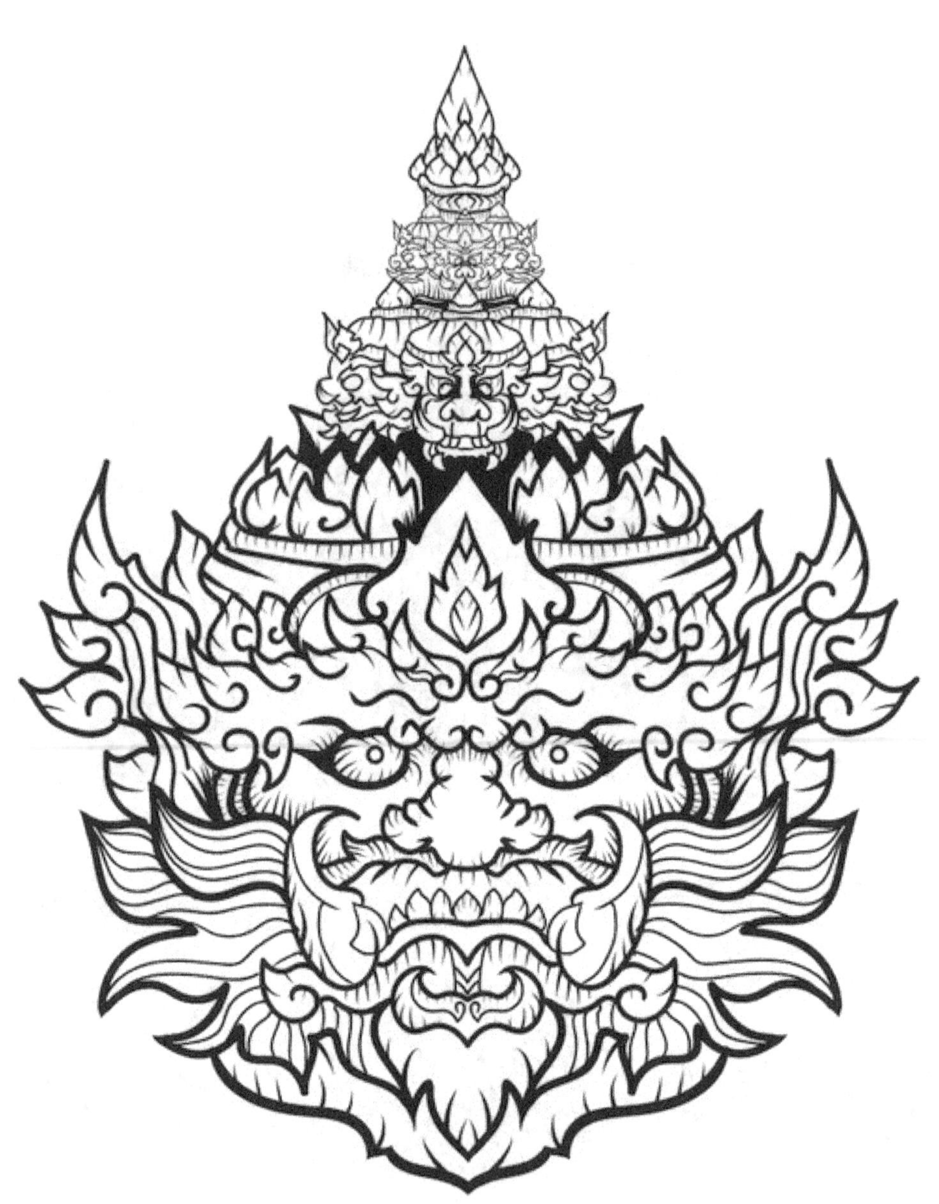

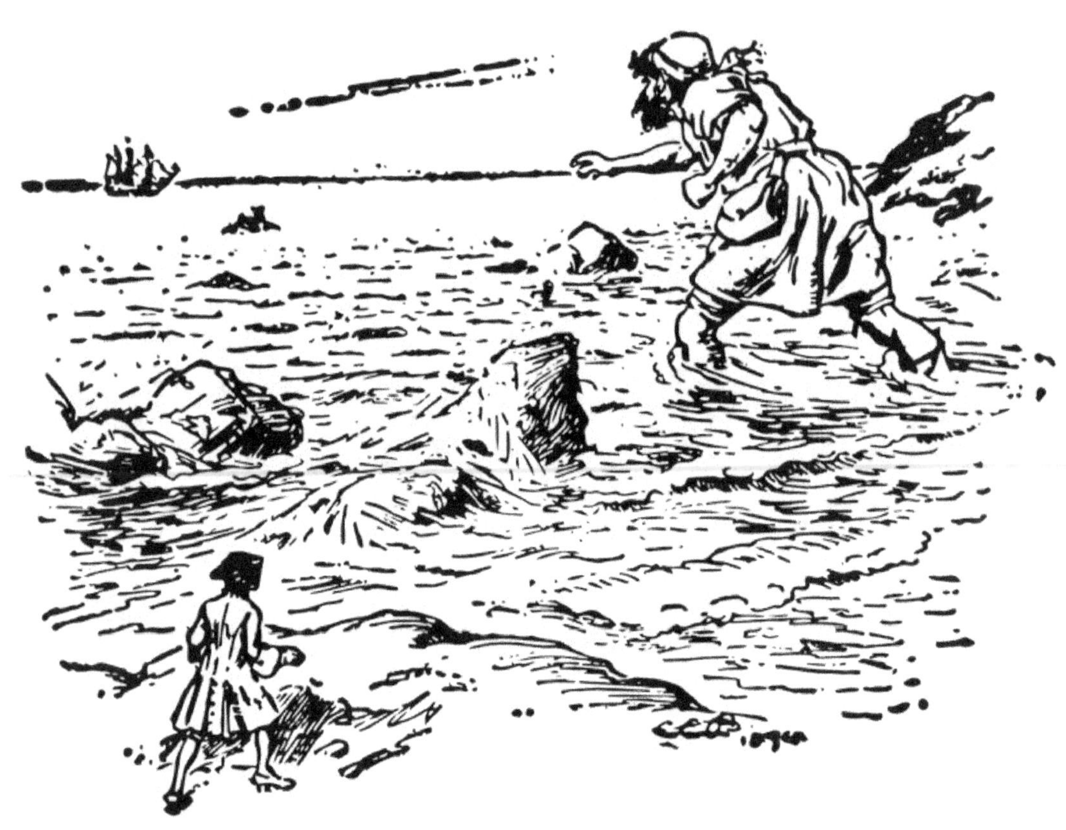

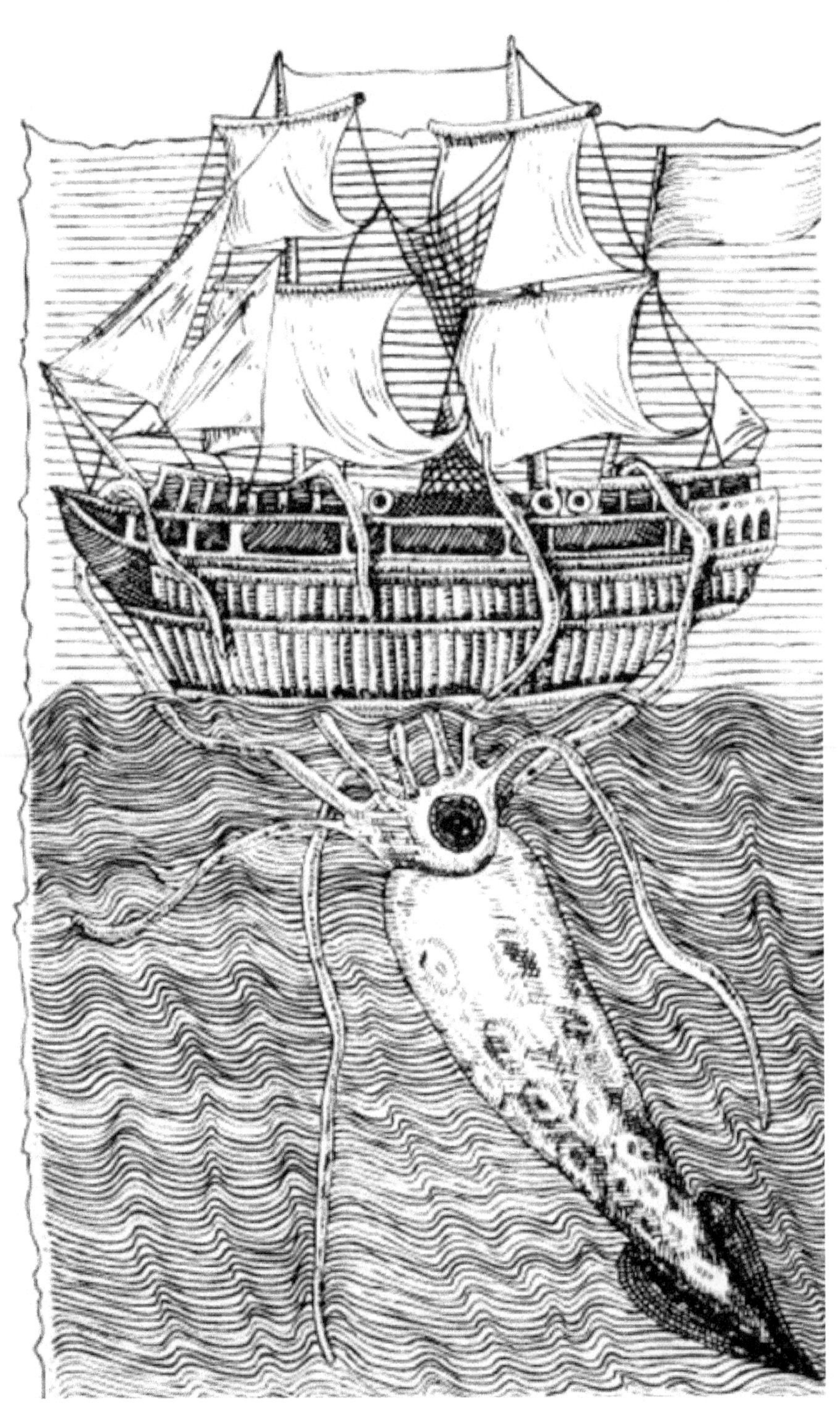

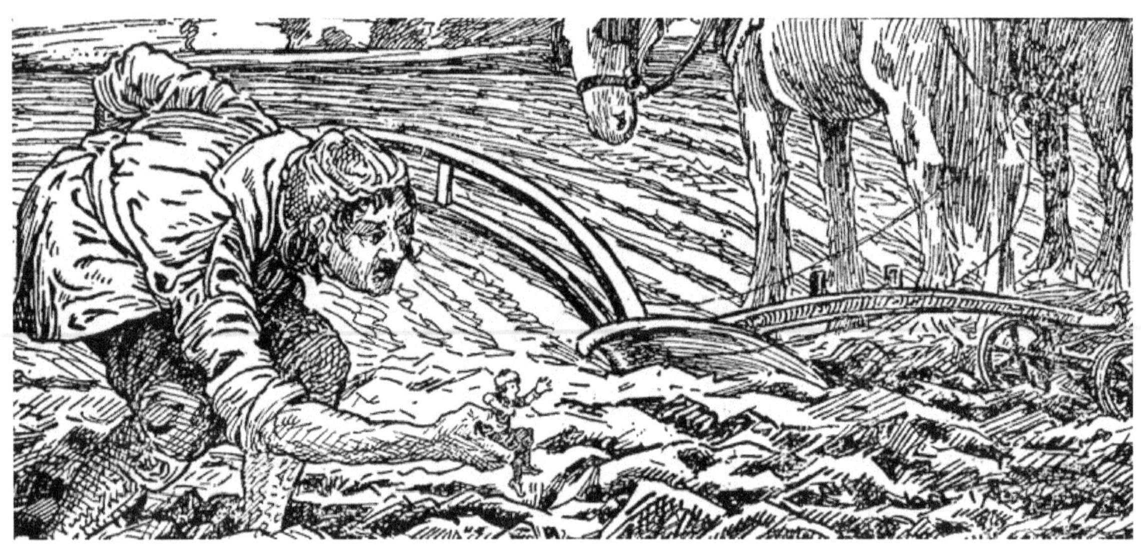

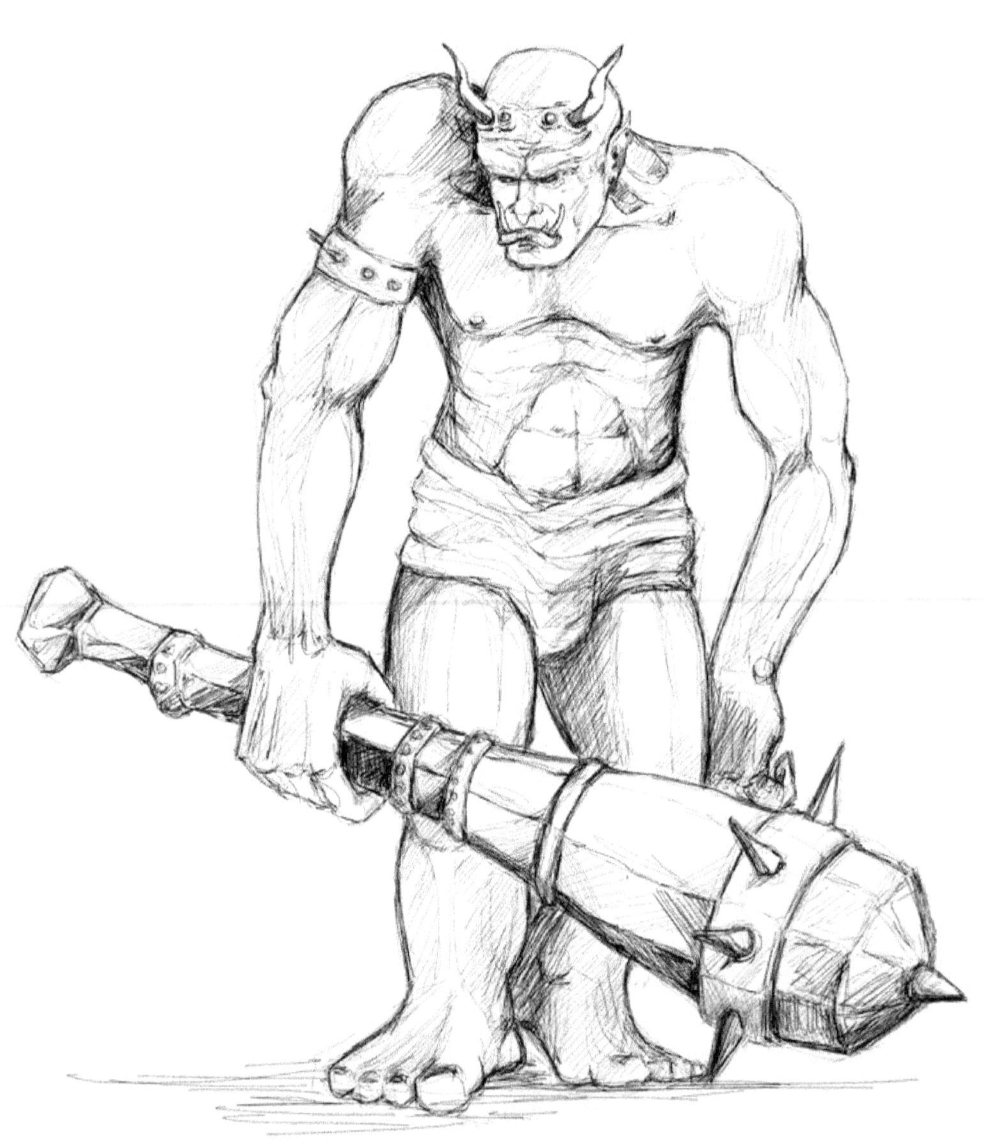

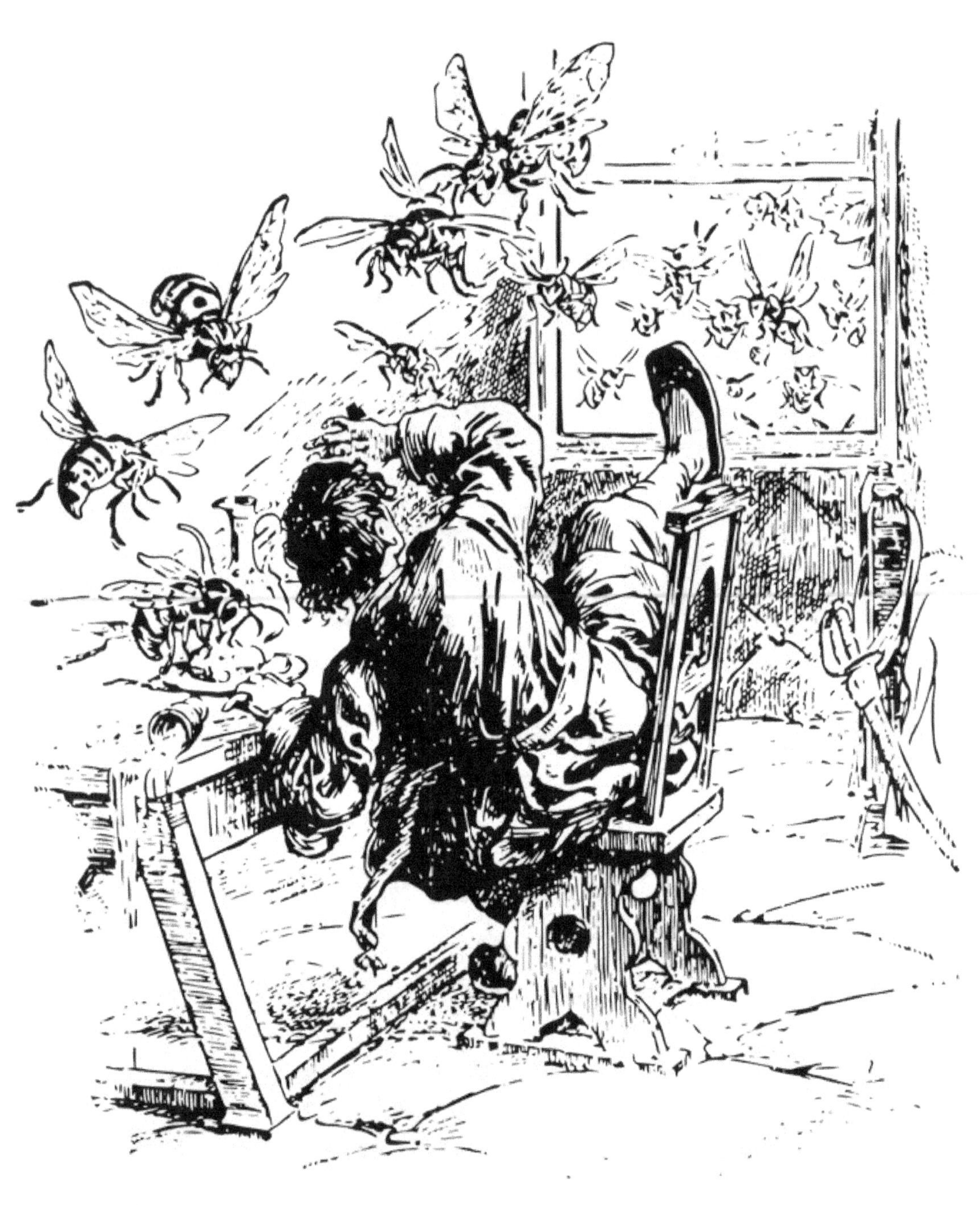

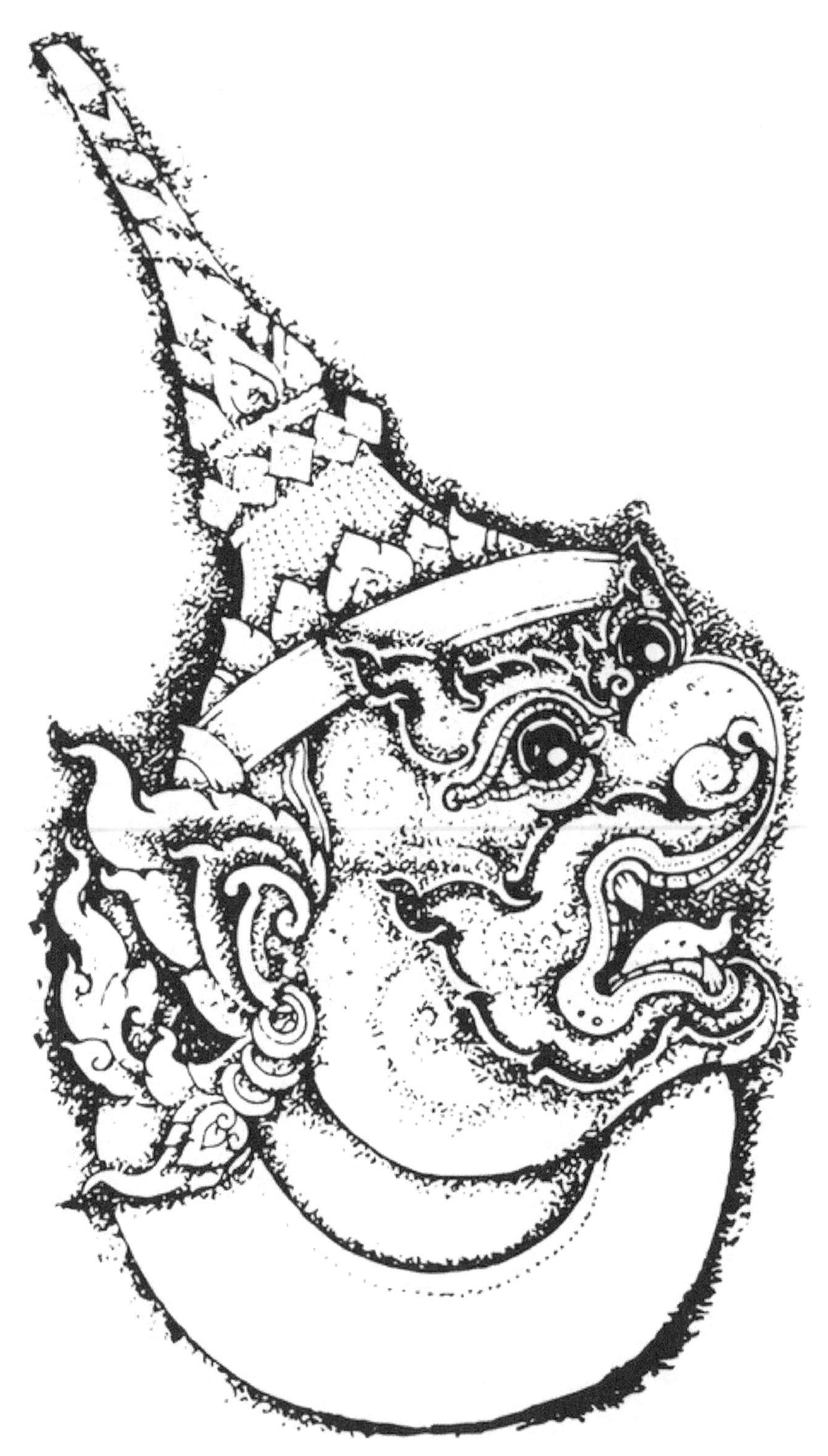

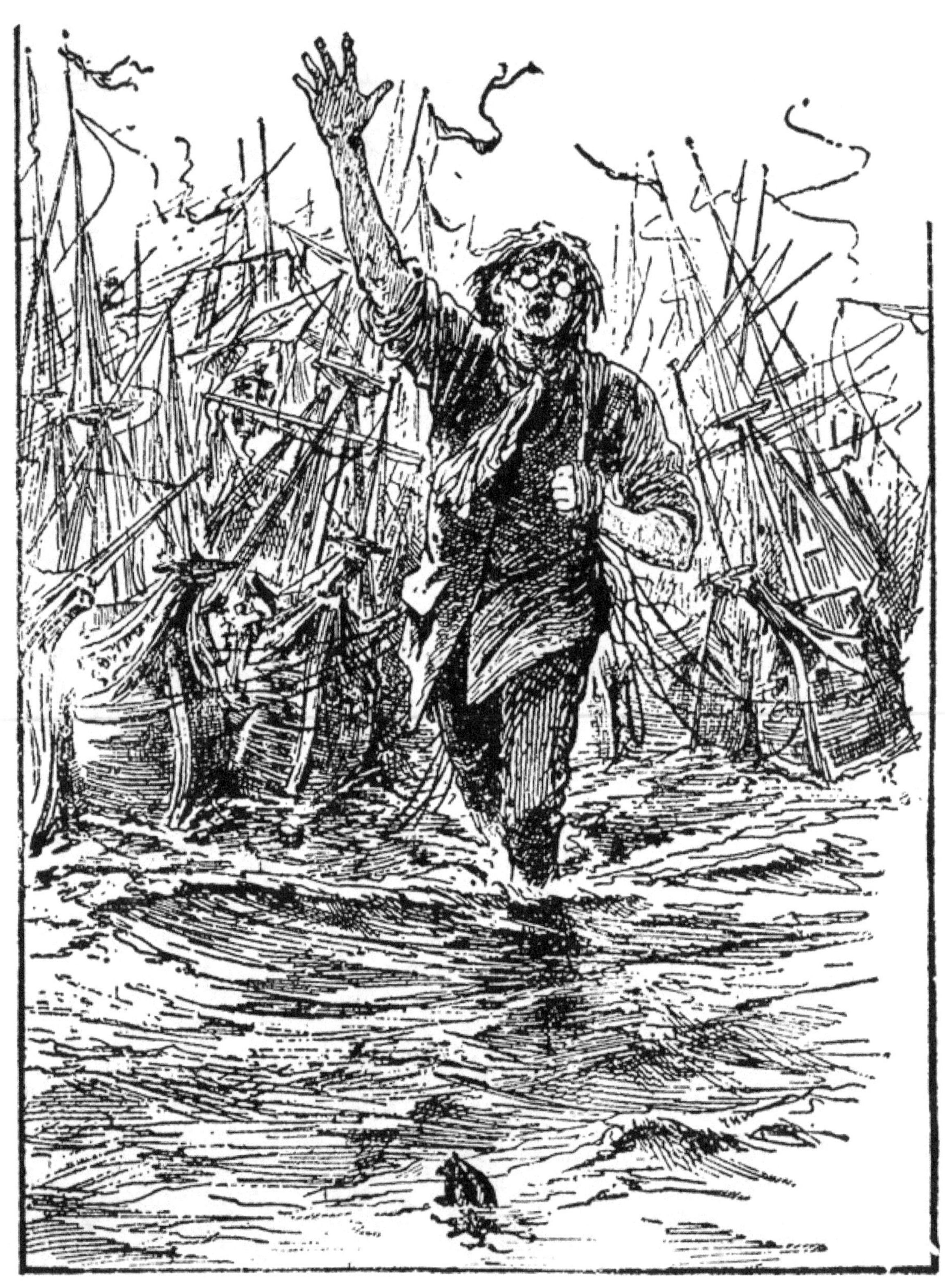

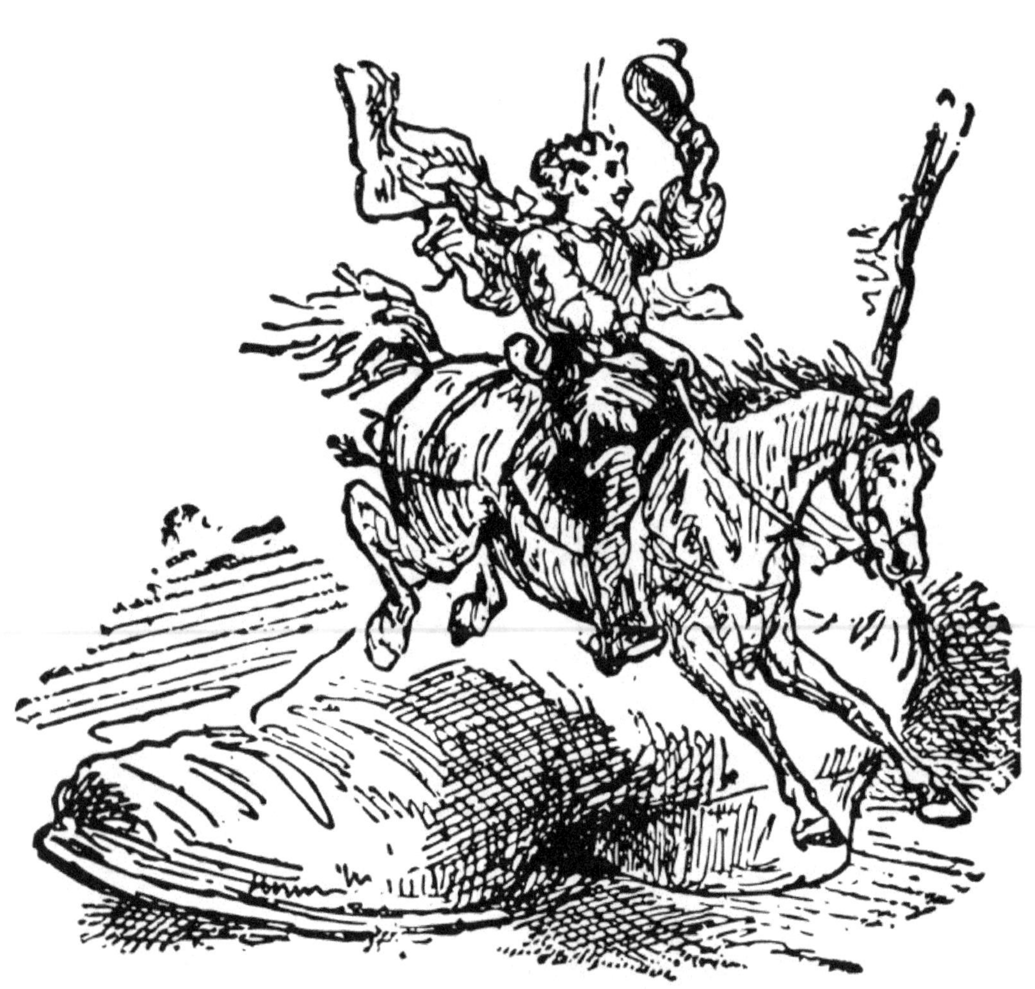

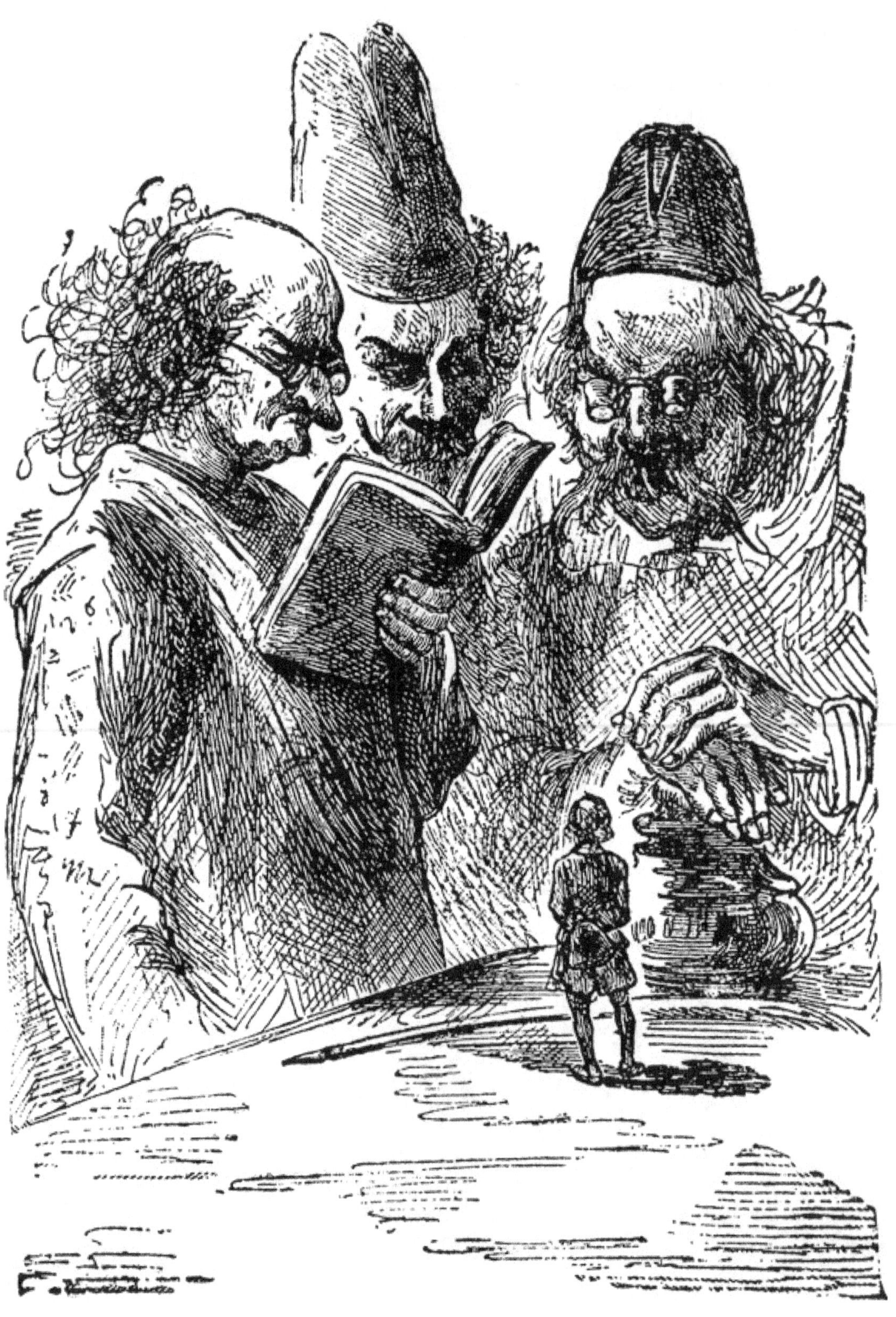

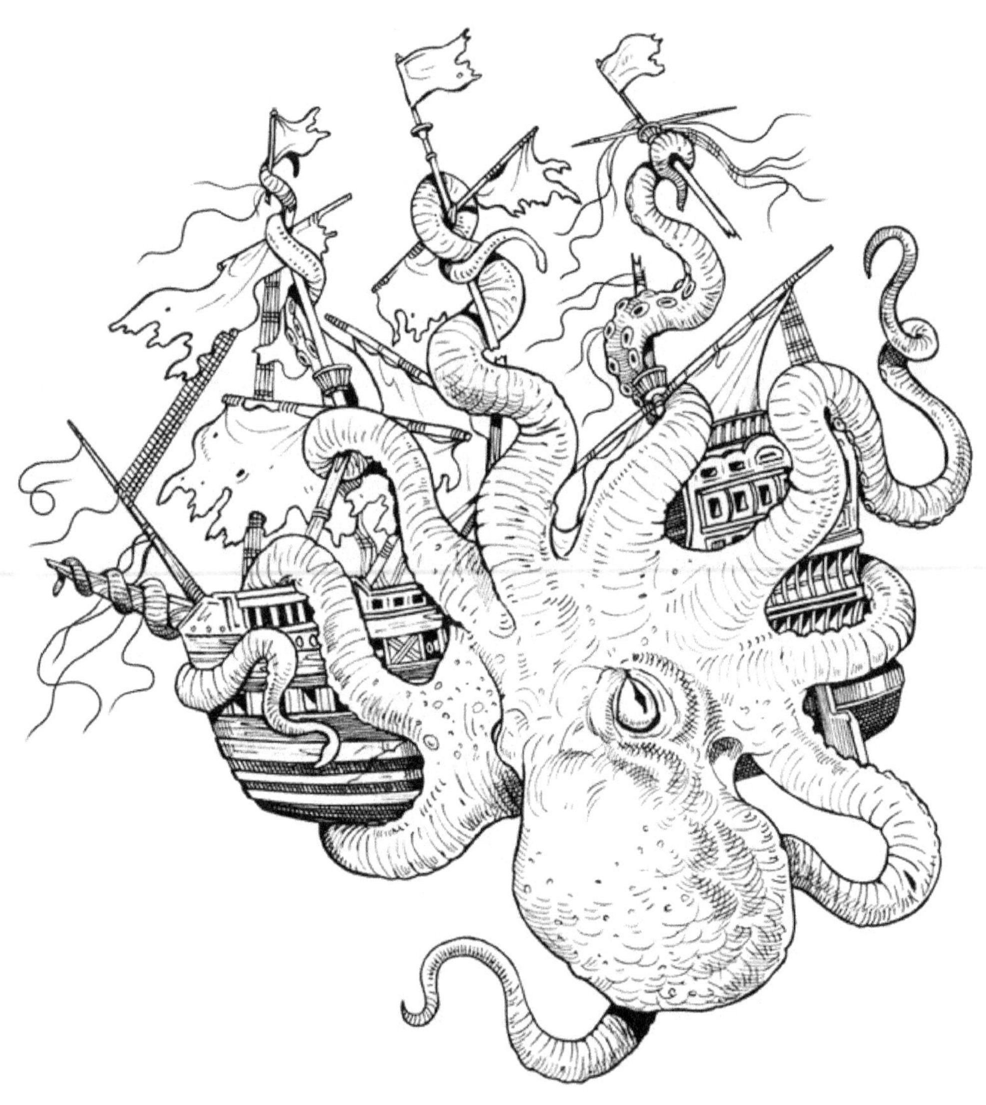

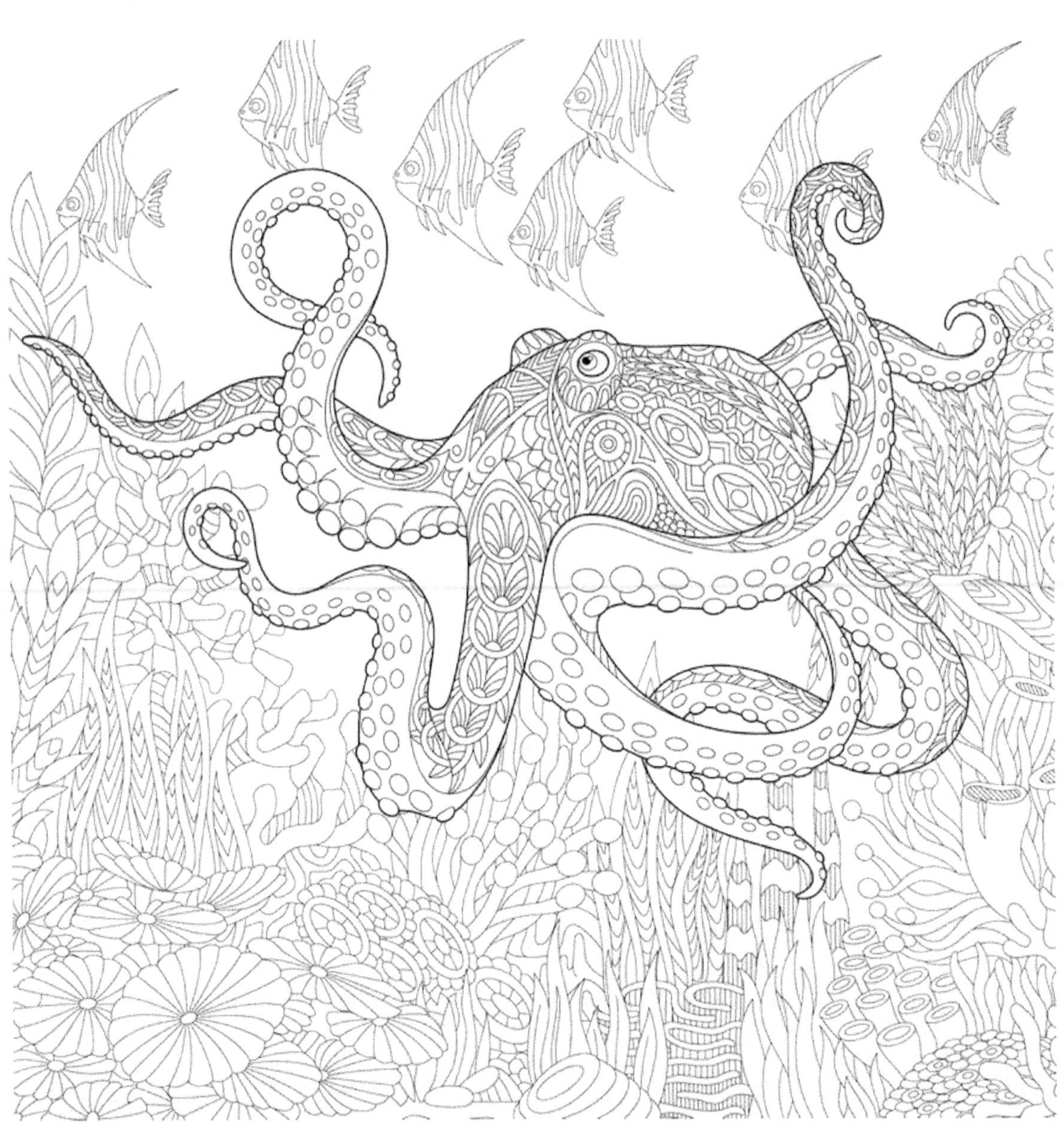

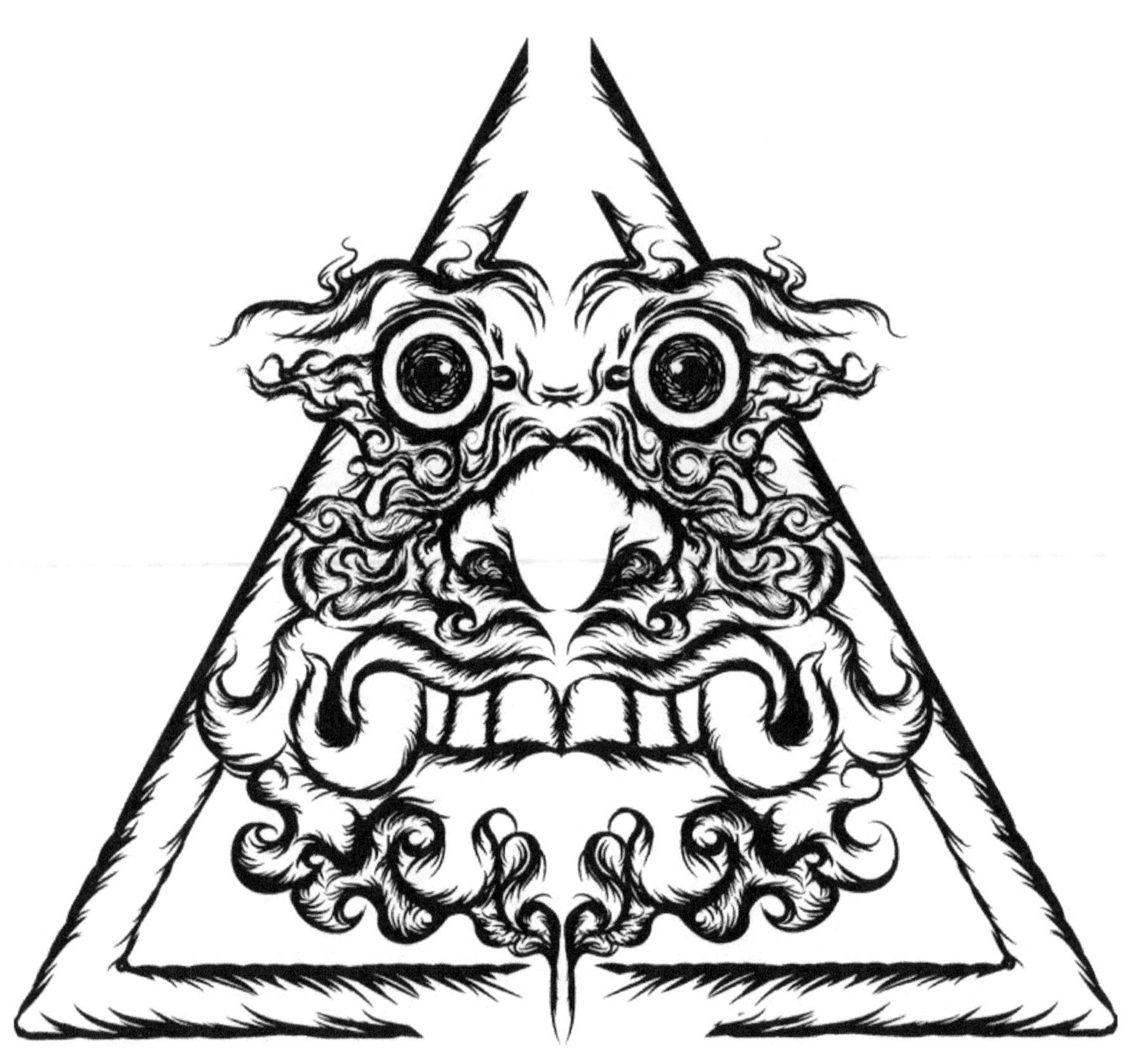

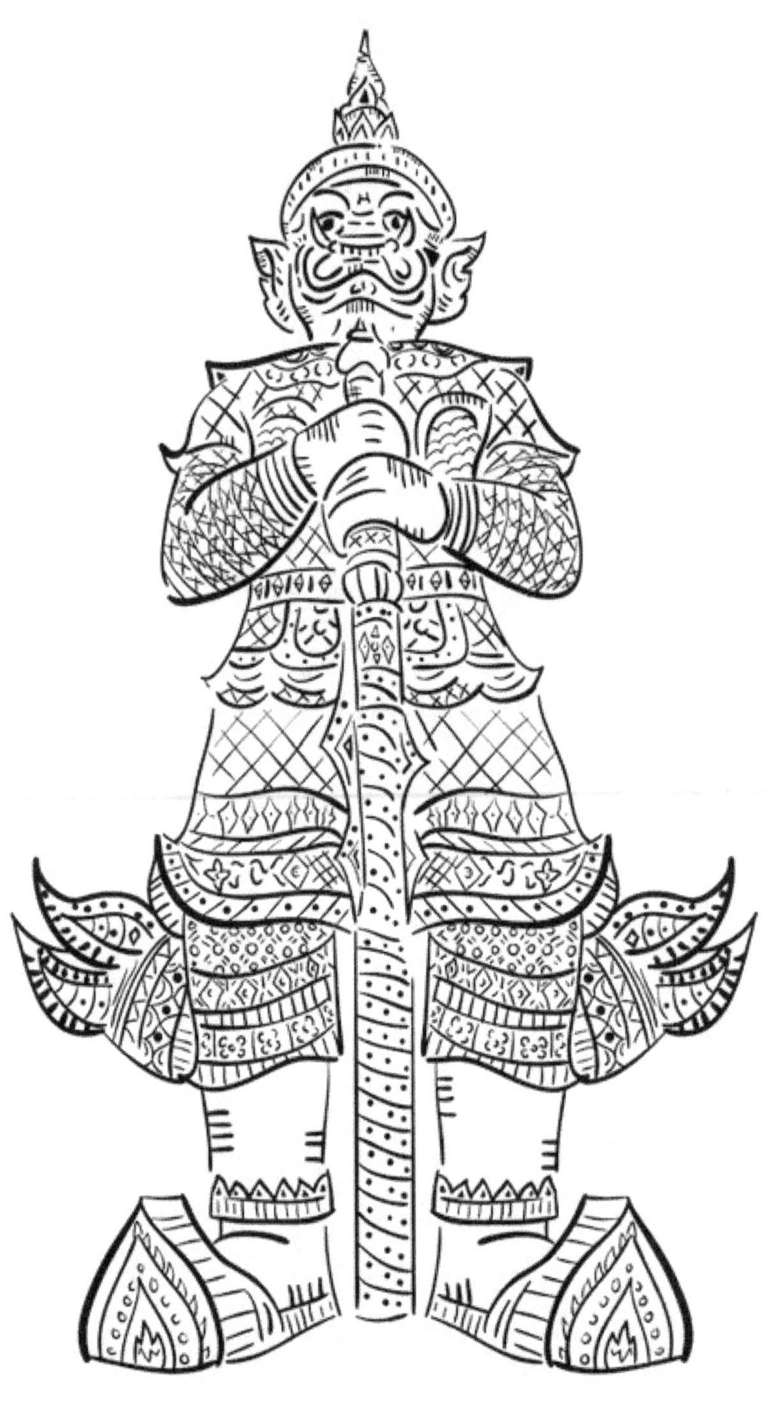

GIANT OF THAILAND

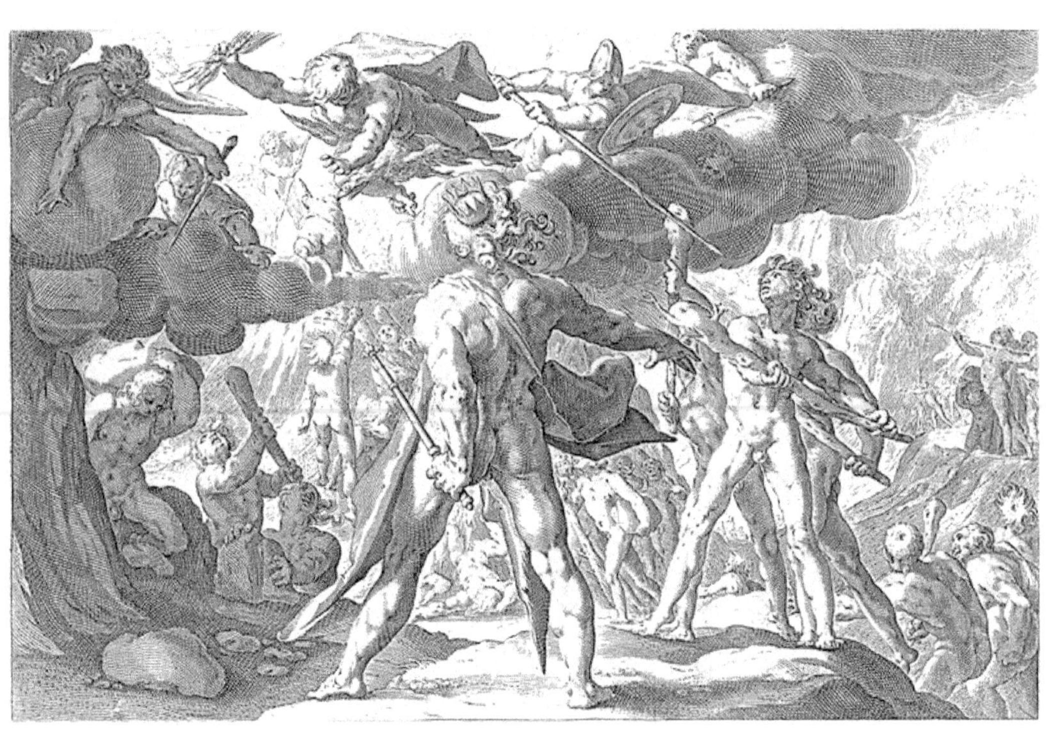

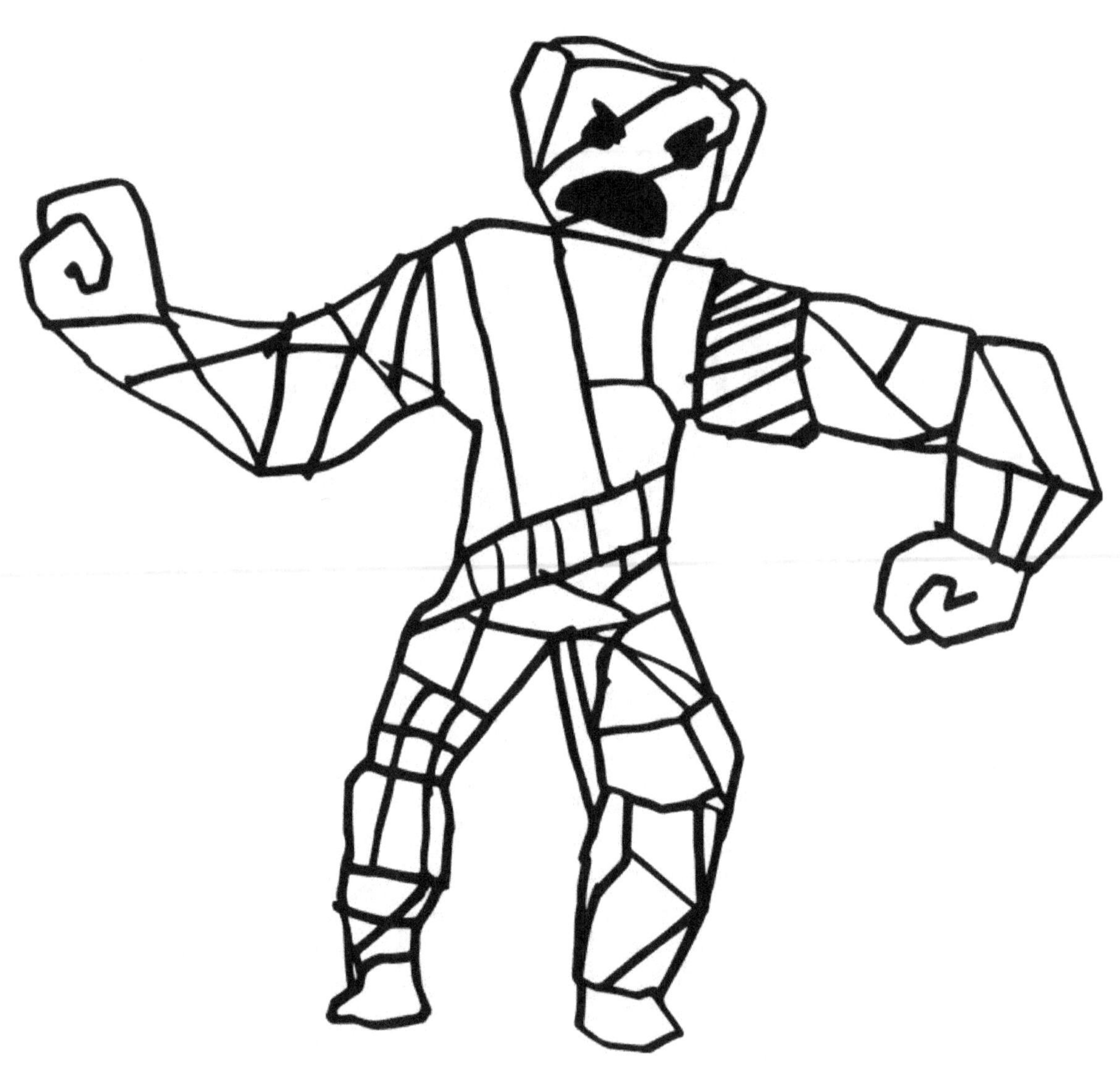

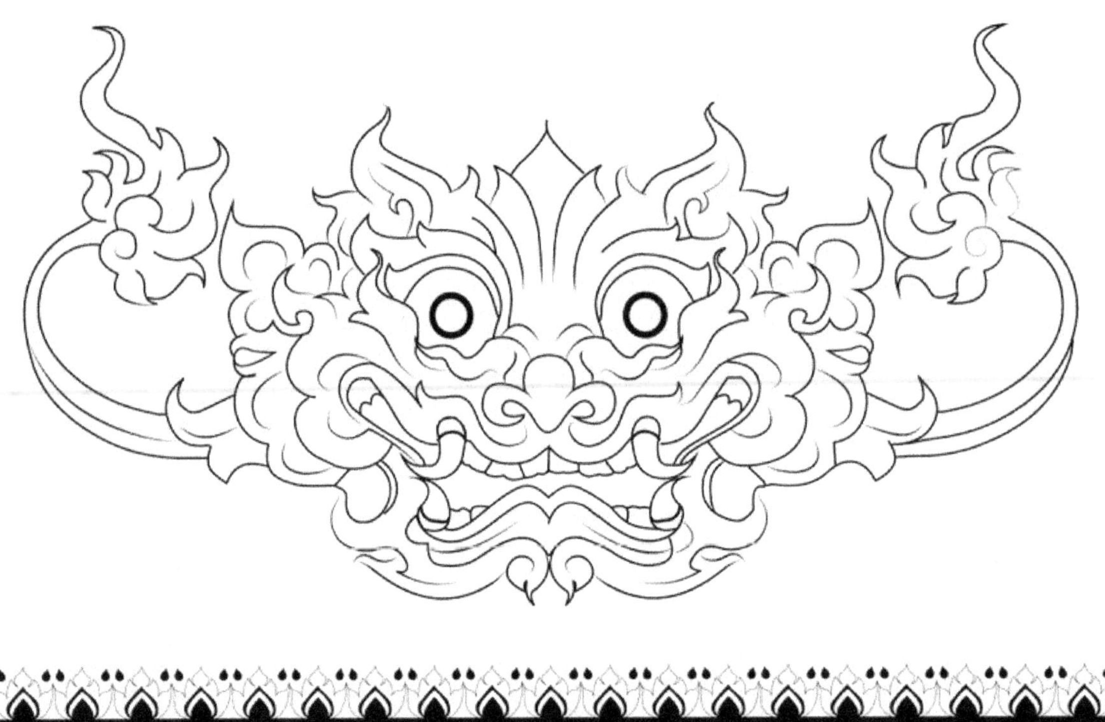

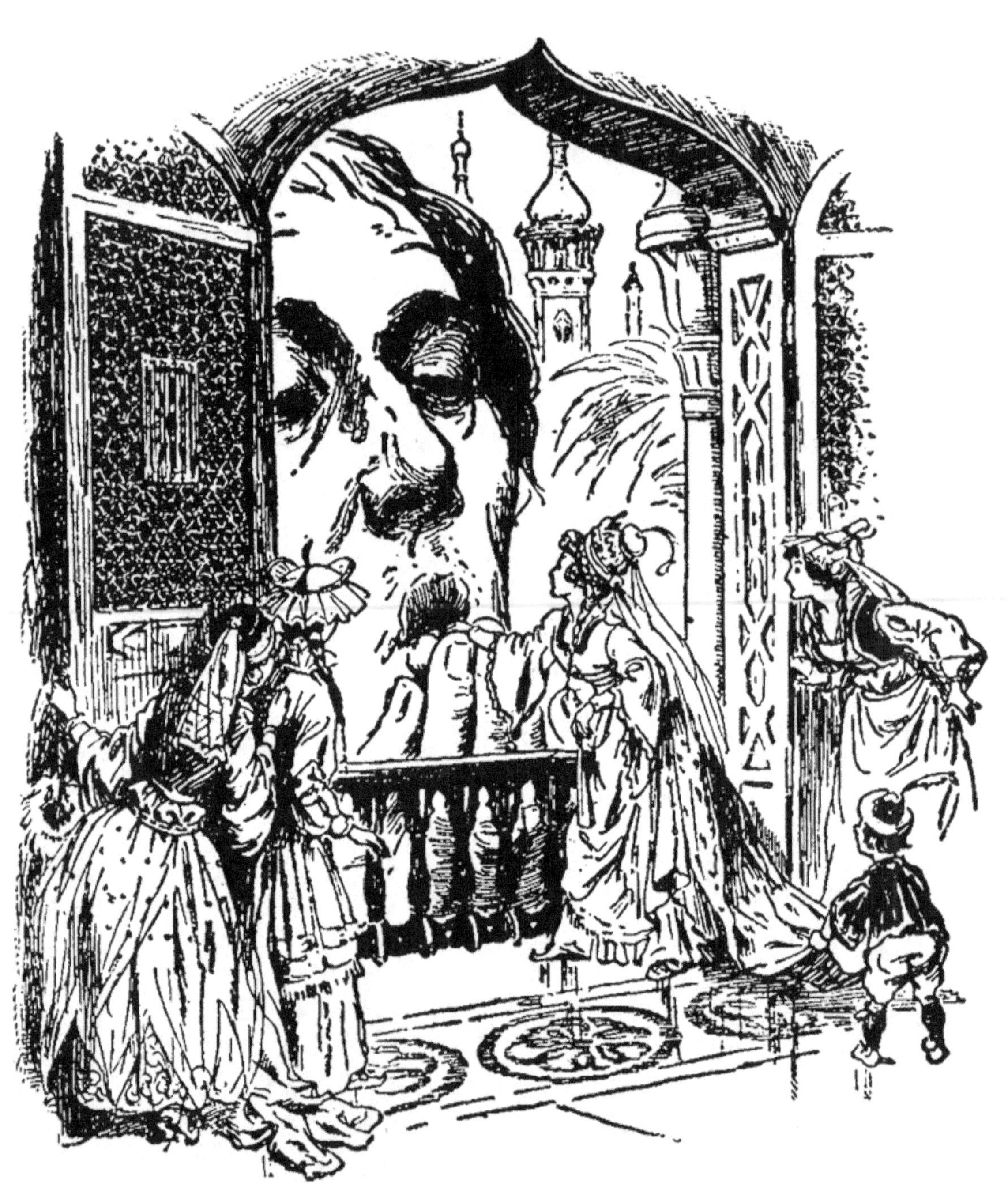

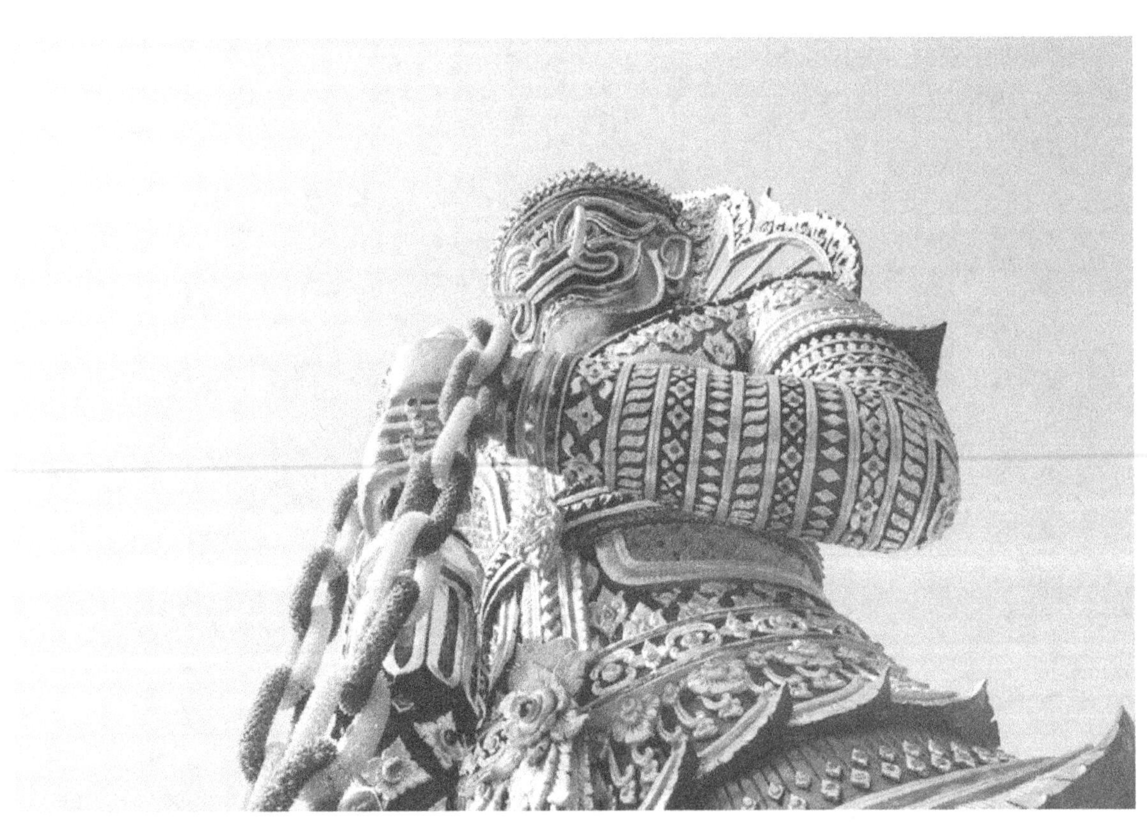

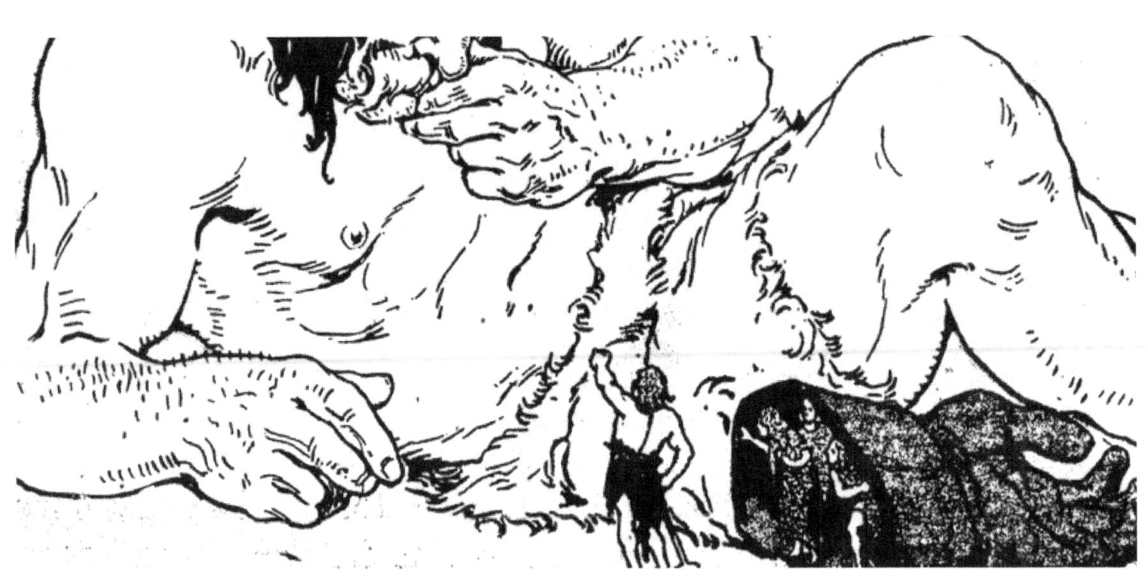

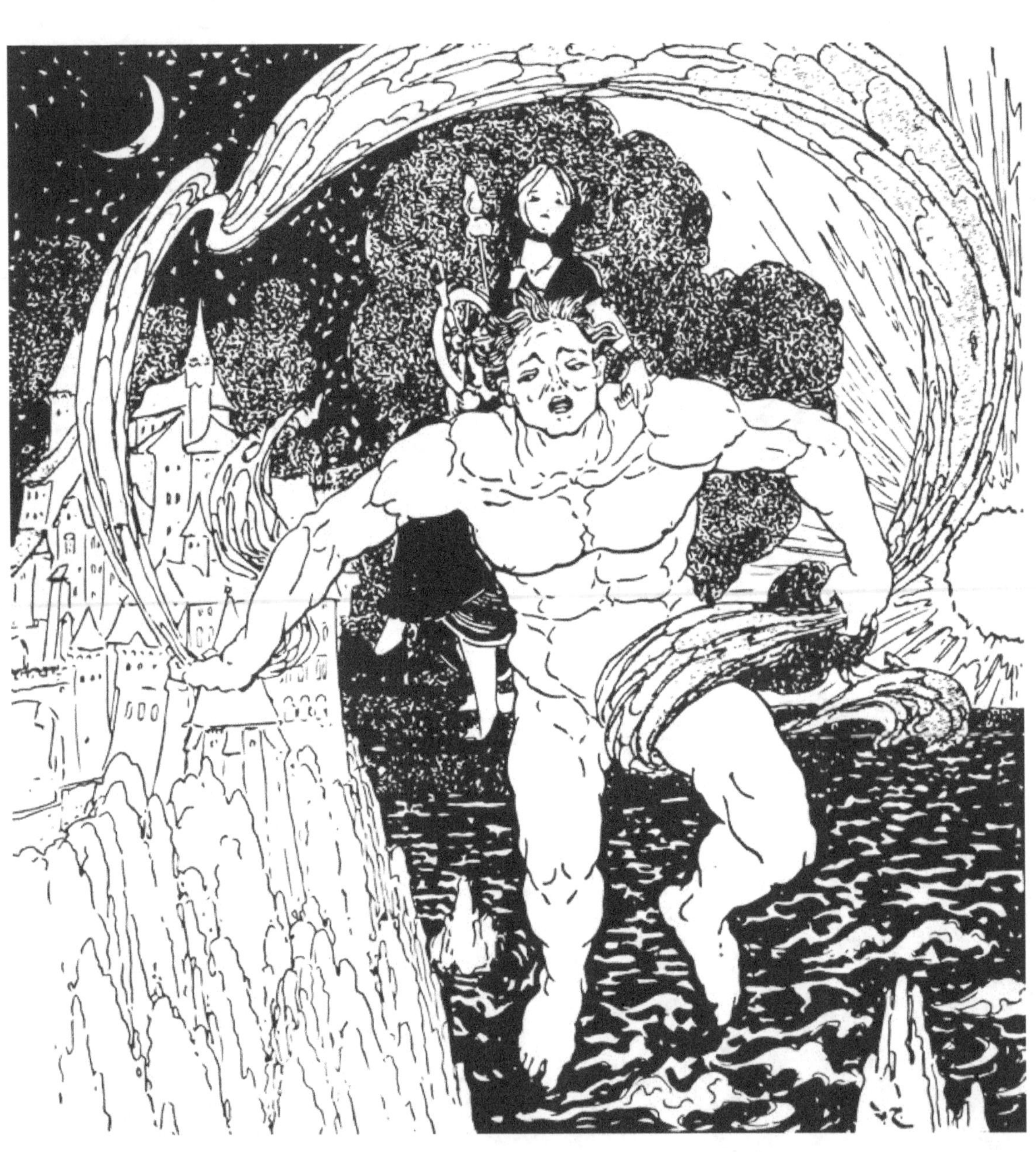

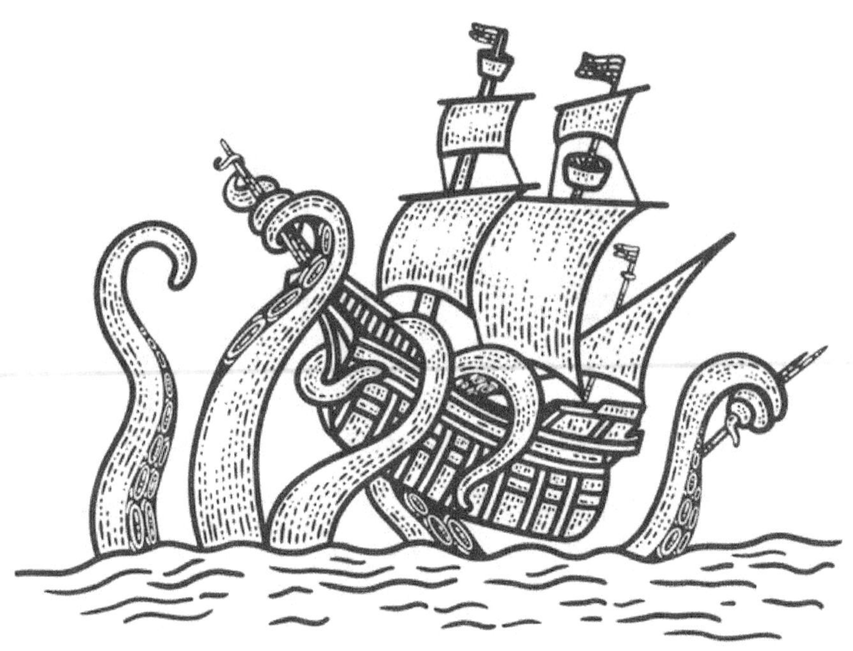

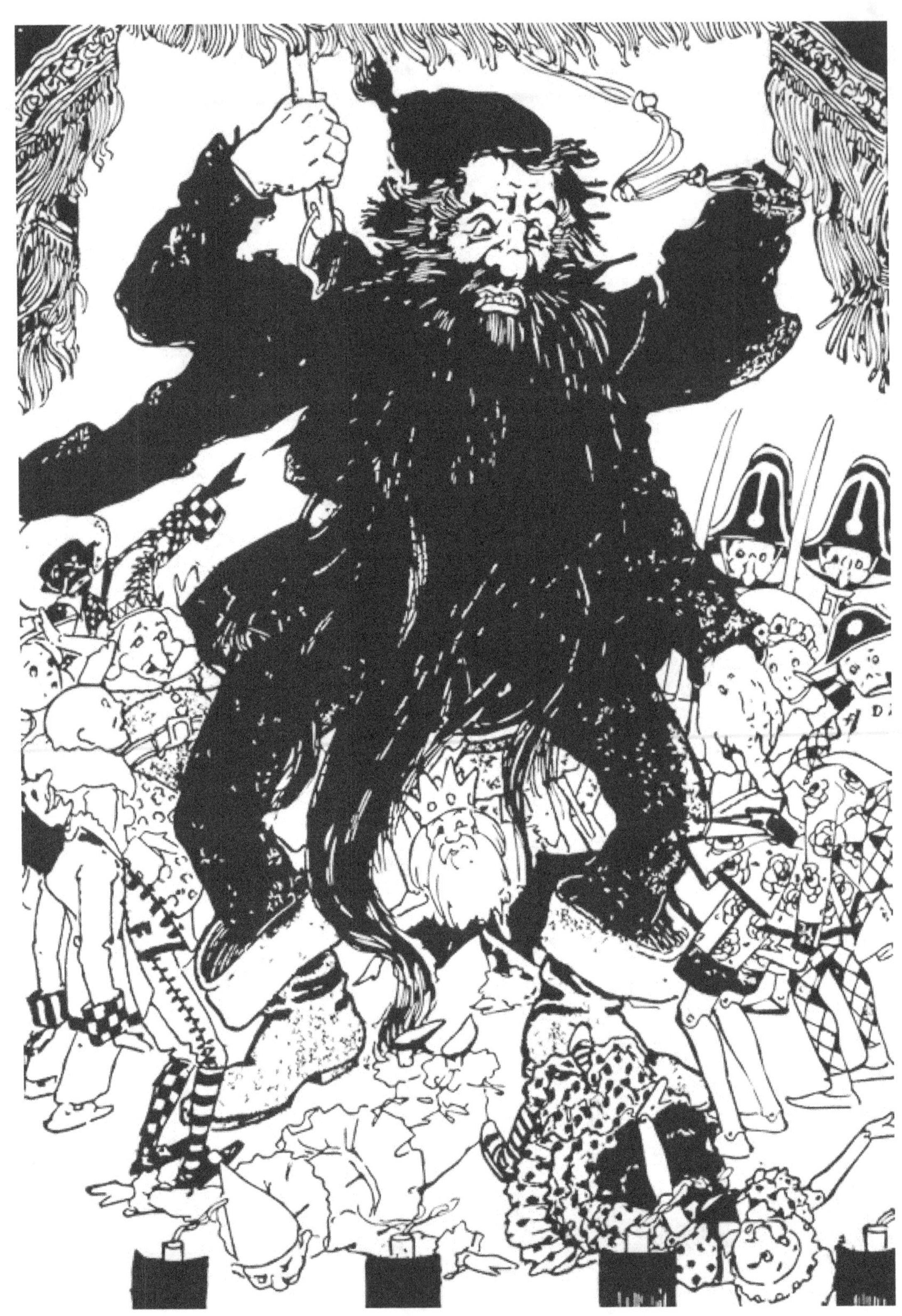

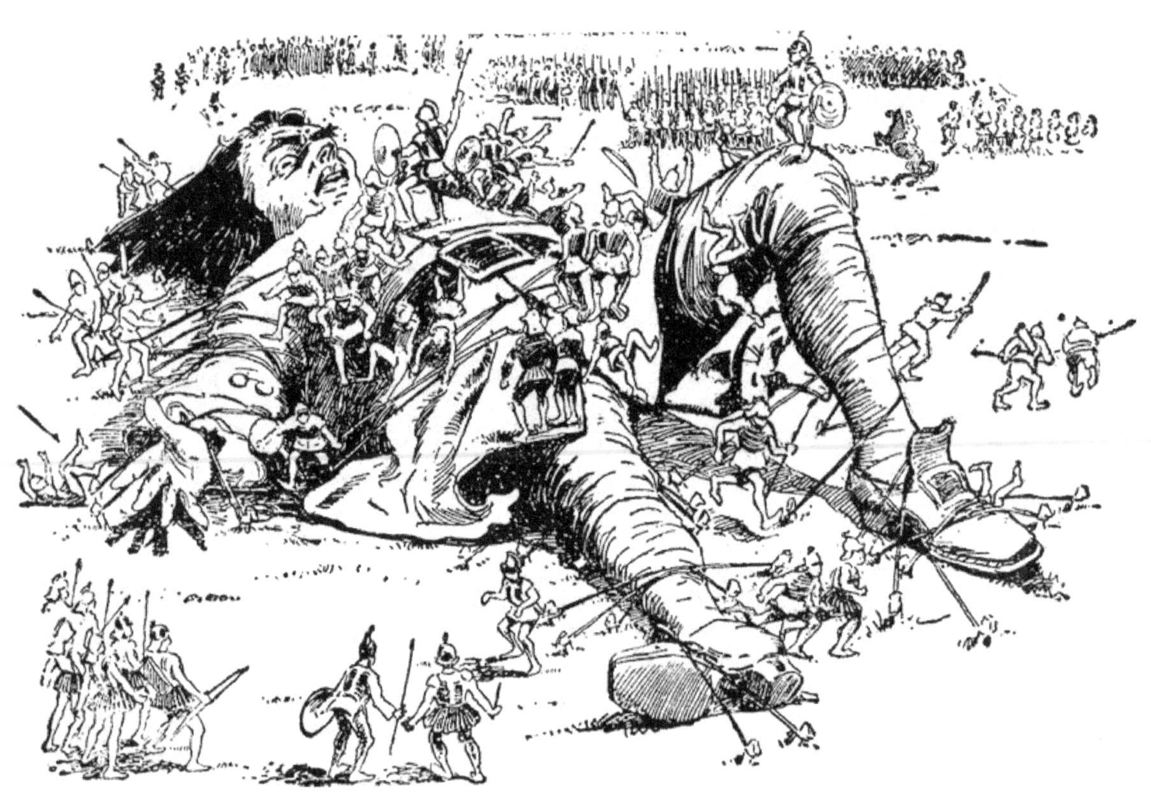

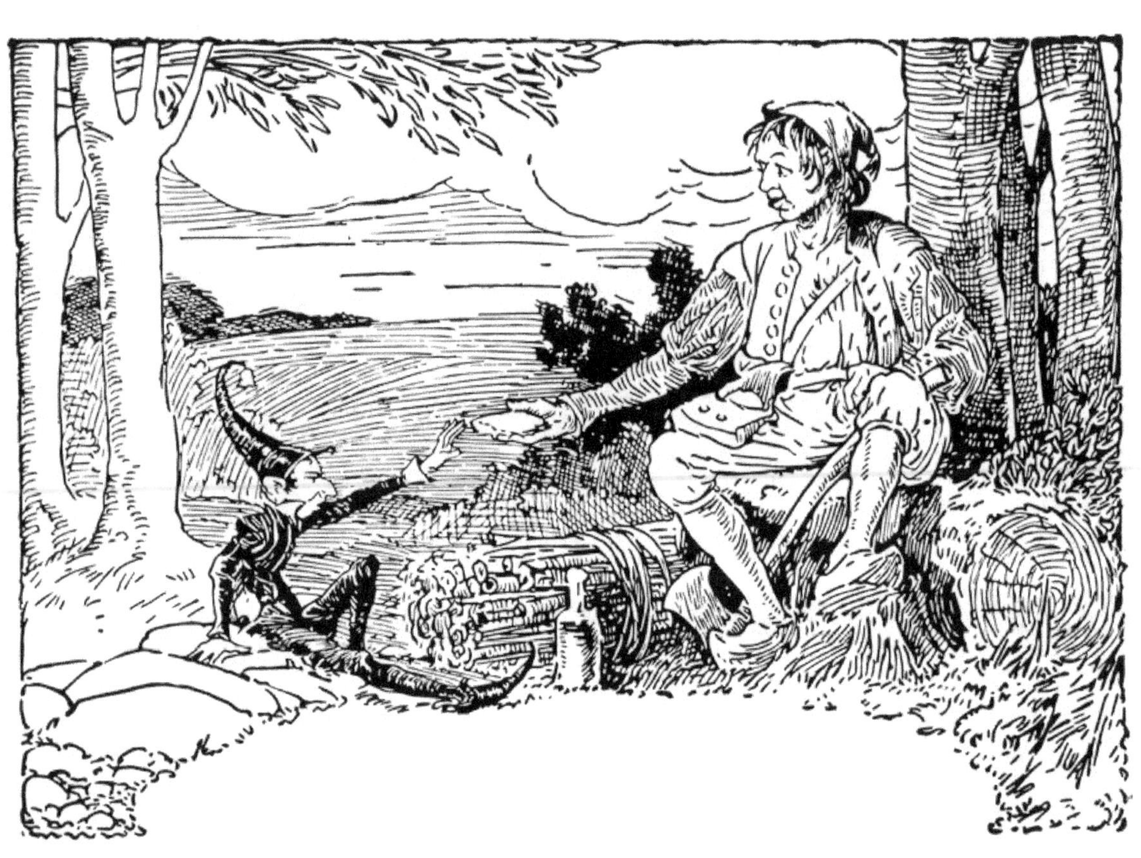

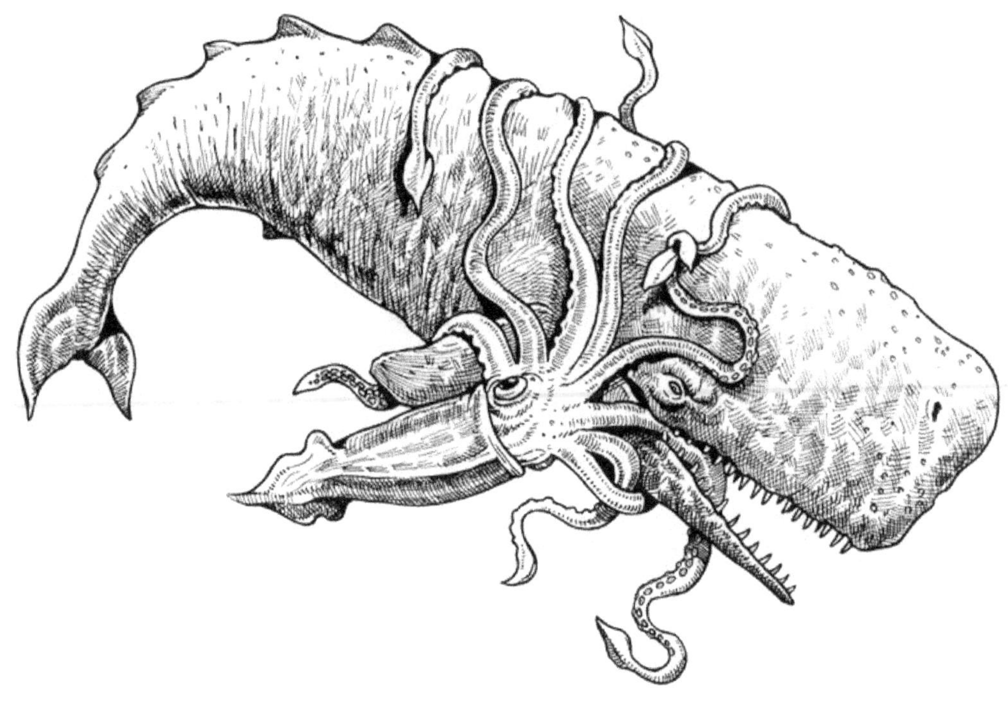

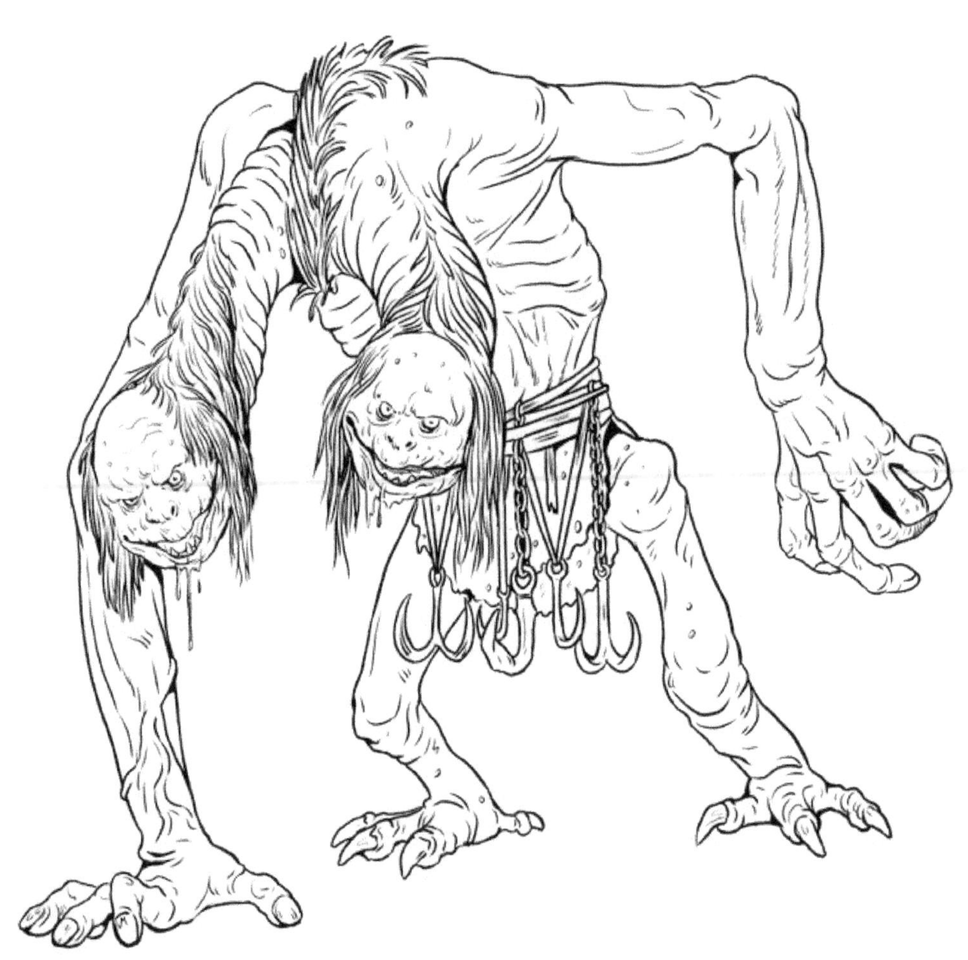

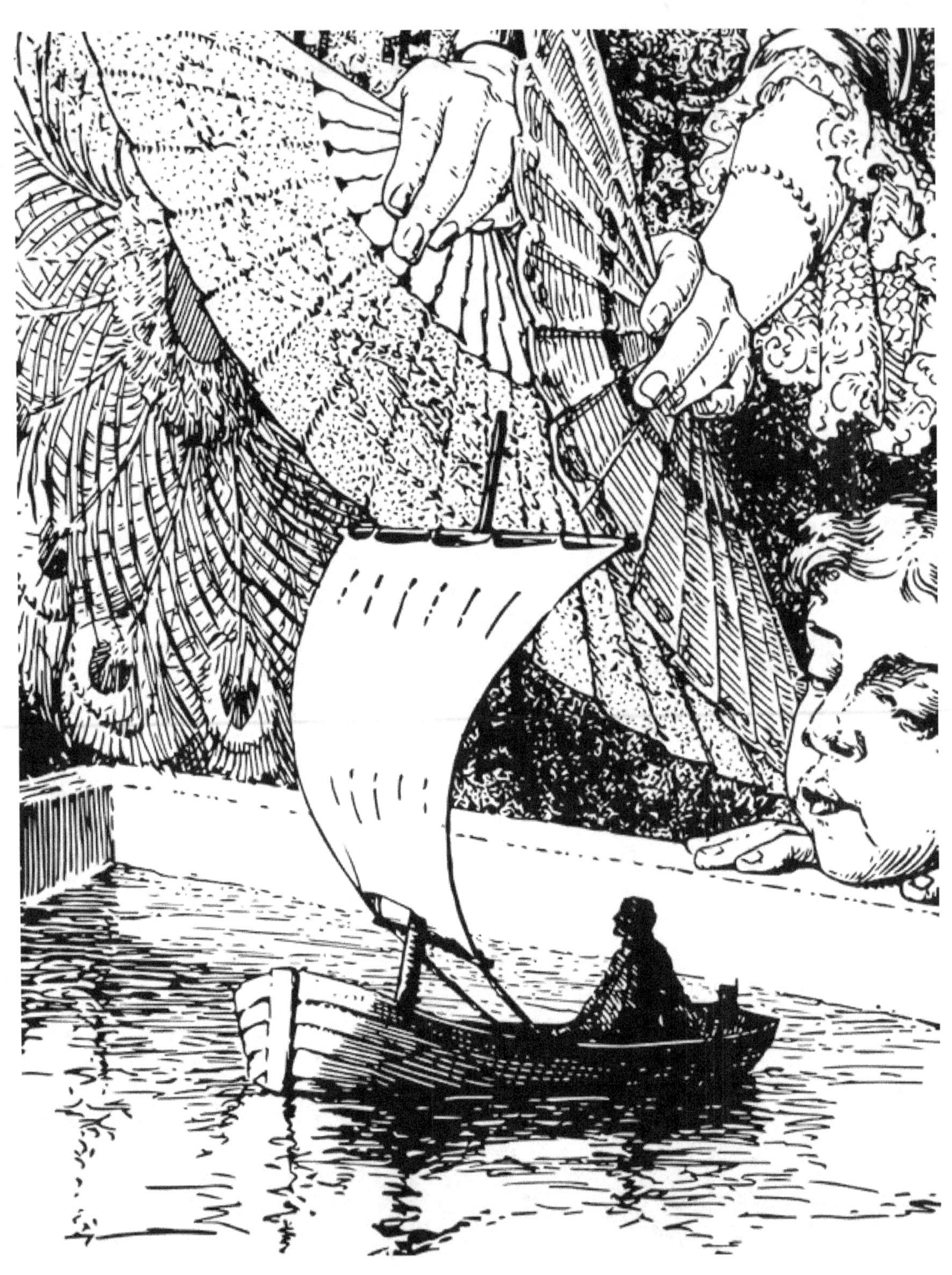

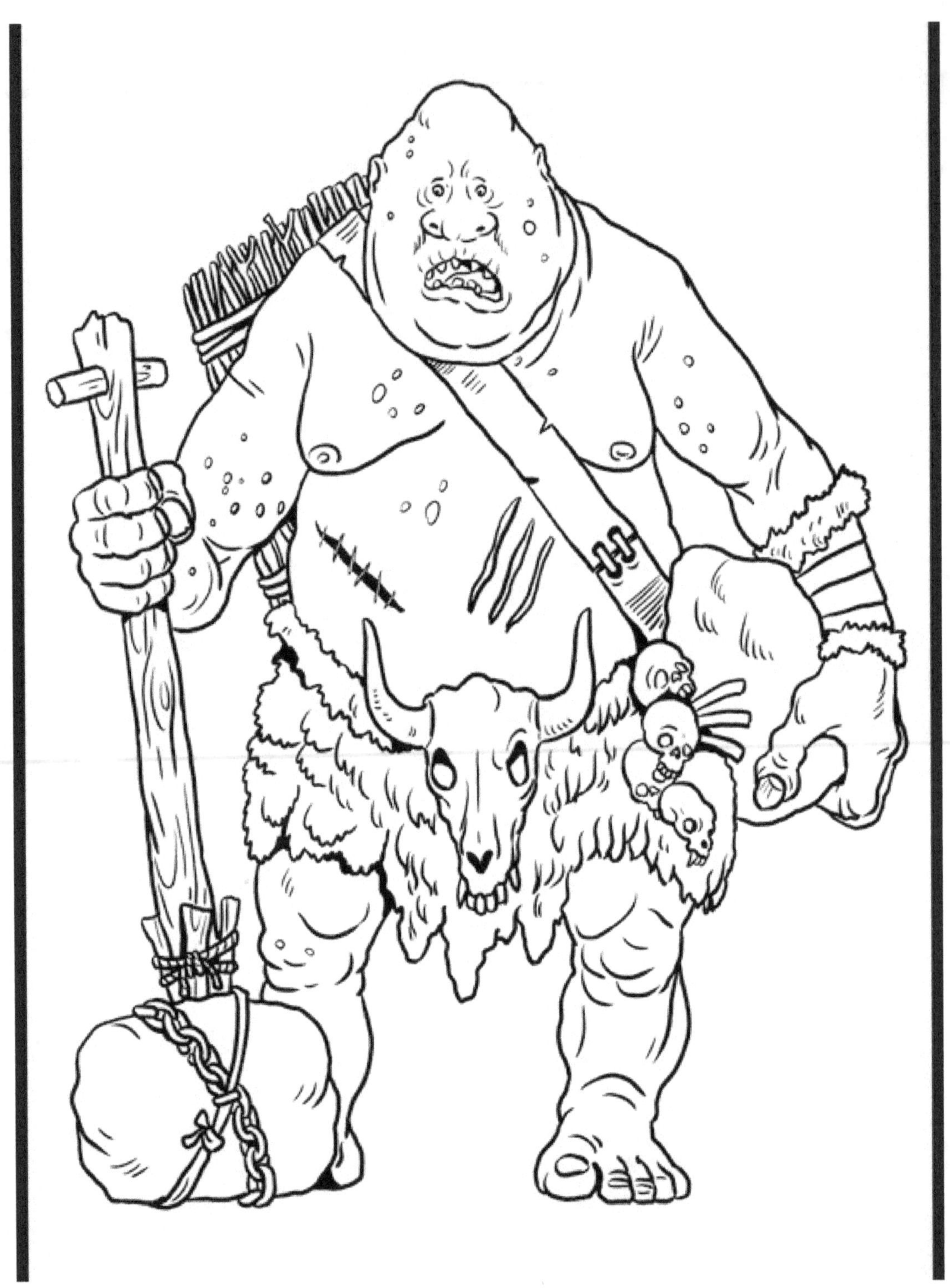

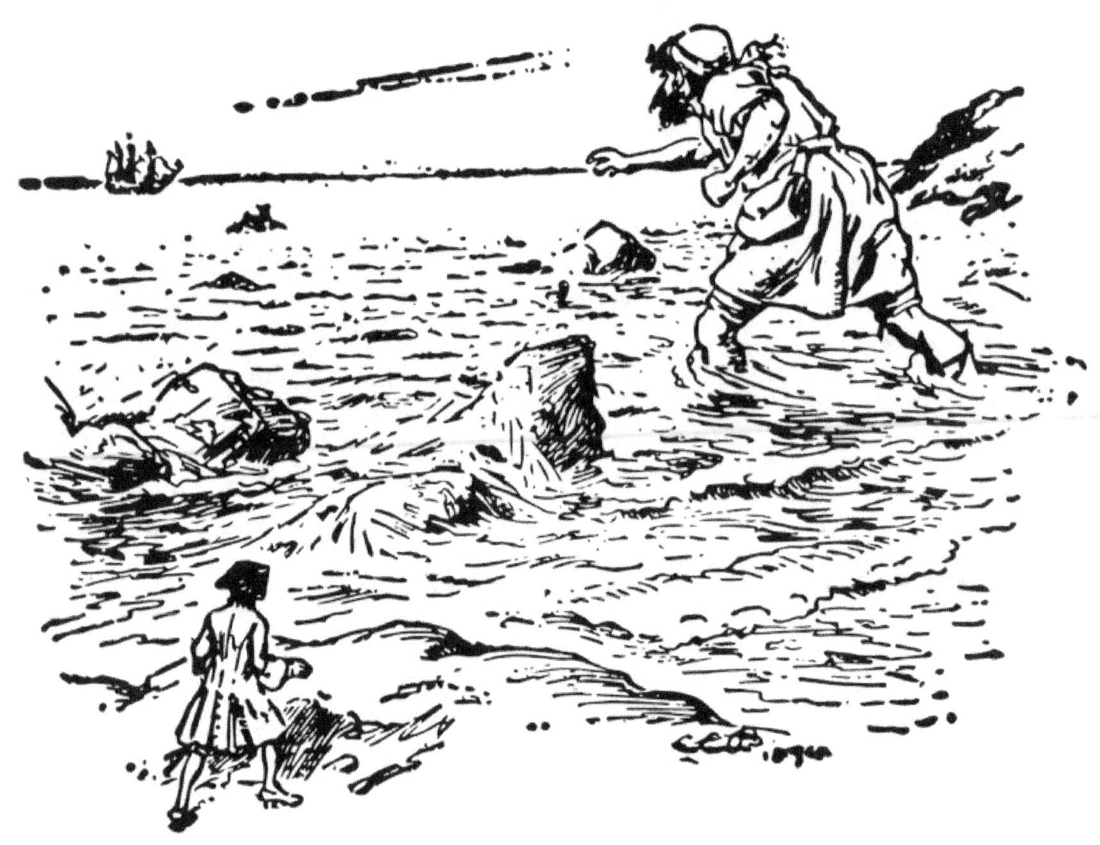

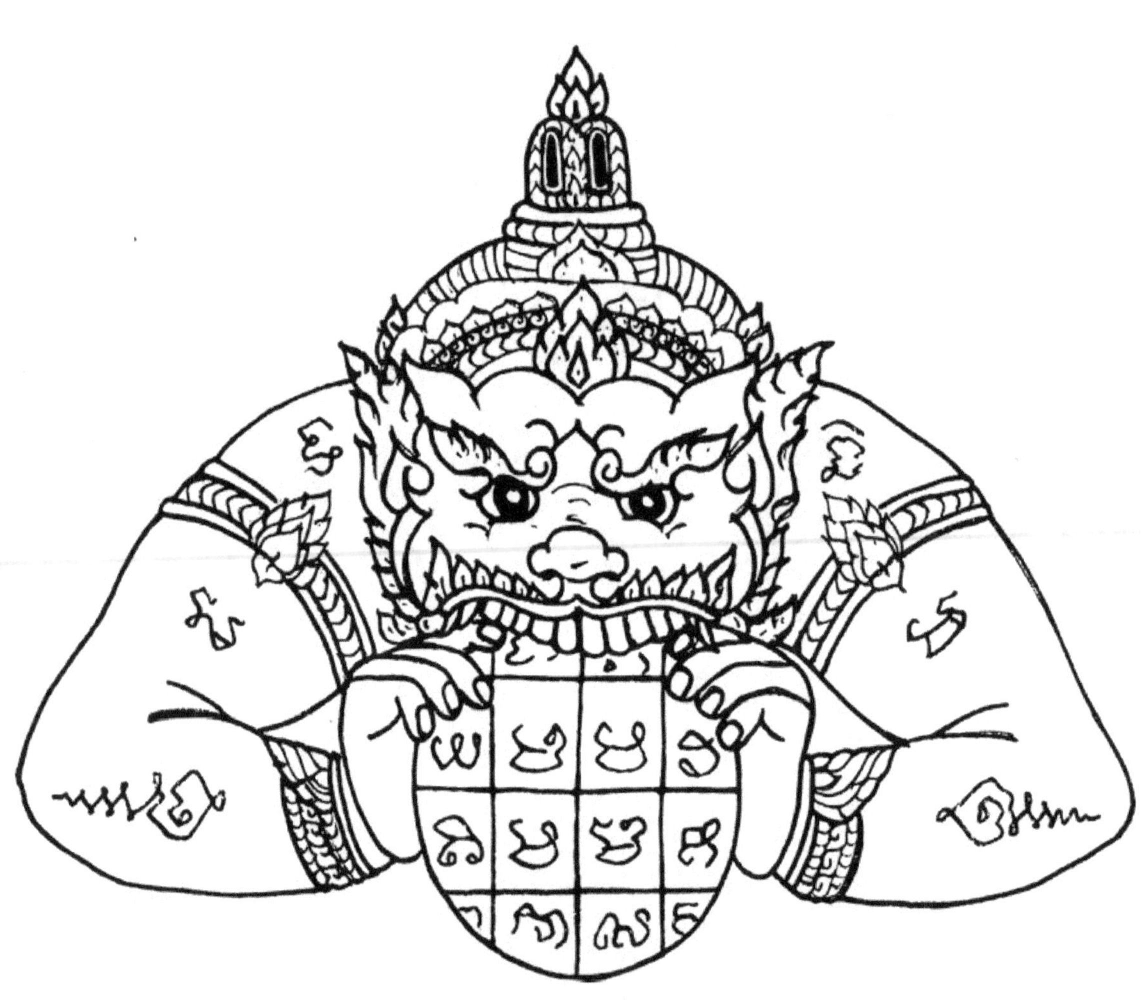

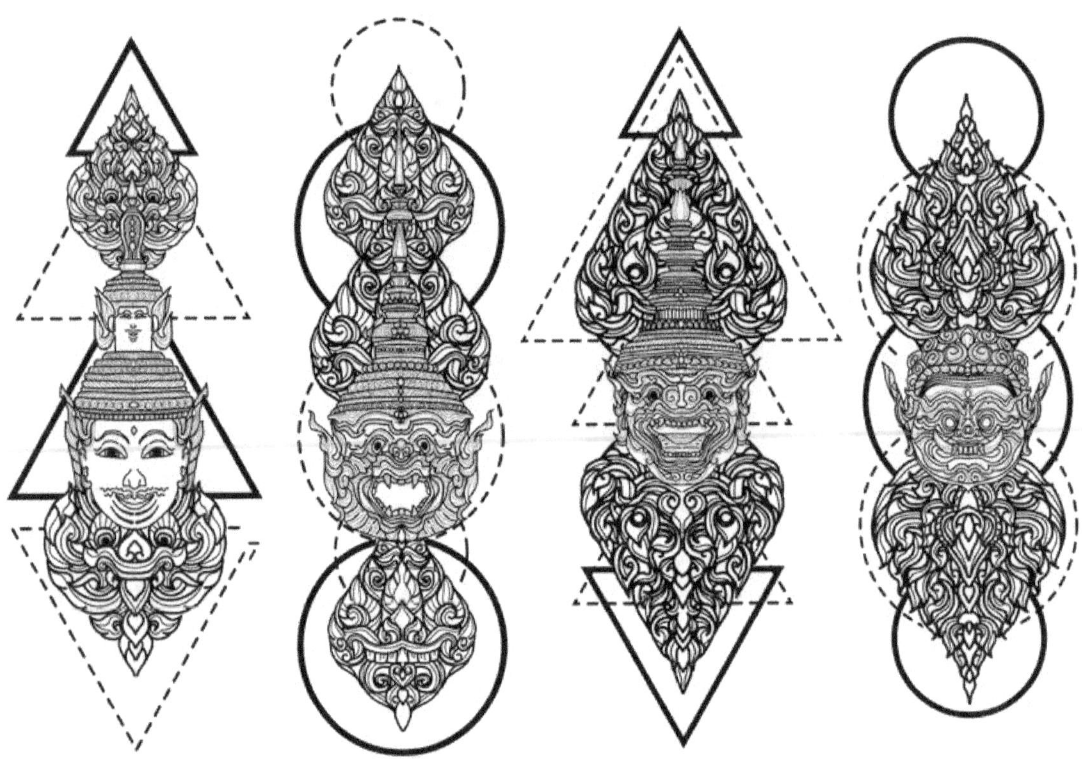

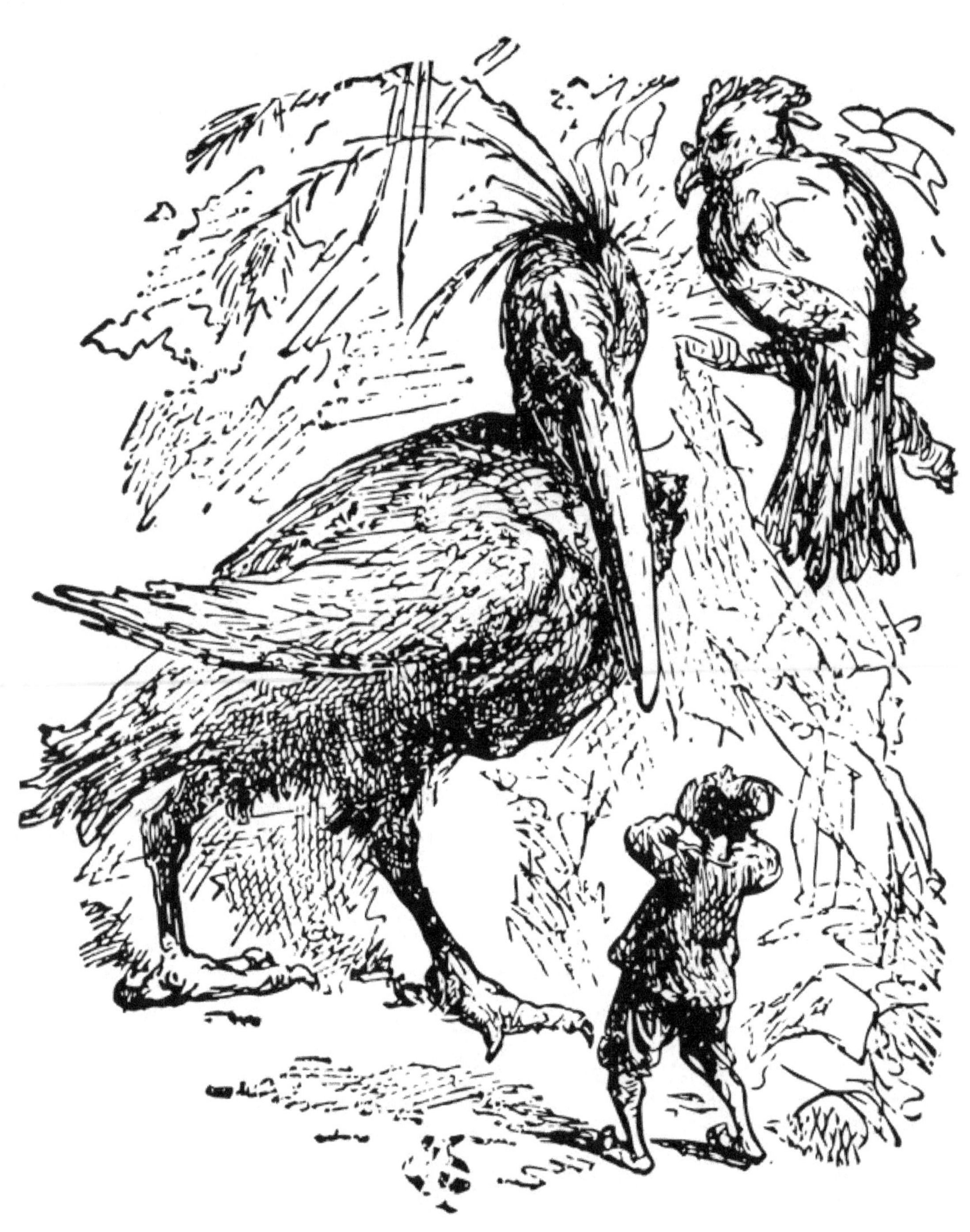